How to Marry a Muslim Girl

Written by s.hukr

How to Marry a Muslim Girl

Publisher: Fajr Noor © 2024

All Rights Reserved

ISBN: 9780645766653

Designed & Authored by s.hukr

Website: fajrnoor.com

How to Marry a Muslim Girl

I pray this book helps all those
Muslim men who suffer in silence.

How to Marry a Muslim Girl

Table of Contents

Must Read 6
A Letter from the Author................................... 8
Introduction 11
You are the Problem! 13
The Grounded Muslim Man 21
    Prerequisite 1 – Accept Islam Sincerely.........................22
    Prerequisite 2 – Meet the Bare Minimum 23
    Prerequisite 3 – Divine Purpose 36

The Ideal Muslim Man 45
    A World of Wealth...47
    Pure Abundance..52
    Respect is Earned..54
    A man of Silent Actions..56
    Believe in Yourself...58
    Never get Comfortable..59
    Responsibilities & Duties...64
    How attractive do you want to become?......................68
    Can men and women be friends? 71
    Awareness...73
    Communication...76

Understanding What Muslim Women Want?.. 78
    Women are from the ribs of Man...................................79
    Women are great Communicators..................................81
    Women love to Talk 82
    Women are not liars...83
    Strengths and Weaknesses 85

Women feel the World 86
Good Women don't ask for much 90
How women see love... 92
Compliments will change her 93
Don't be Yourself... 94

The High Value Muslim Woman 99

Not all women are the same... 100
What to look for? 102
How to find her? 105
Green Flags 108
Red Flags... 115

How to Marry a Muslim Girl? 119

Requirements of Nikkah 121
How to approach her?... 123
Getting to know Her... 126
How to test Her? 128
Be Dominate and Decisive 130
When to Commit.. 132
Coffee or Tea?... 134
Conclusion.. 142
Do you want my help?.. 143

Must Read

You may be tempted to skip to the chapters that interests you the most. Don't.

Fight that temptation.

This book has been carefully written in a particular order and rewritten so that you will not jeopardise your own success.

Trust the Process.

This book is no ordinary book. It will challenge your beliefs about life, women and Islam. There may be times when you disagree with me and want to stop reading.

That's a Good Sign.

That is how you should feel. I want the truth to hurt and sting, to make you question everything. Ultimately you will use that energy and achieve exponential growth.

Pain is a catalyst for Growth.

Now it's up to you, will you use this book to live the life you dream or will you allow fear of something other than Allah to hold you back? The choice is always in your hands.

How to Marry a Muslim Girl

Remember…

Allah does not change the condition of people unless they change what is within themselves.

- Quran 13:11

A Letter from the Author

How to Marry a Muslim Girl

ٱلسَّلَامُ عَلَيْكُمْ my dear brother,

We live in a world that is ever changing, that has become so difficult to navigate especially as Muslim men living in the west.

I find myself surrounded by weak men who have no idea on how to establish and maintain healthy relationships, especially with their women – Mothers, Sisters and Wives.

Perhaps I could help by share some valuable lessons and knowledge that I have learnt on my journey. That inshallah you can benefit from and add great value into your life. I hope my work inspires a generation of Men to become attractive in every sense of the word.

This book is to serve as a guide on how you can strive towards certain ideals to become a man that is admired, loved, and respected.

Inshallah, this book will give you the ability to marry any Muslim woman so effortlessly. While the goal is highly desirable and simple to understand, it is by no means easy. This book will challenge your beliefs and your inner reality.

Nothing good in life comes easy, so please have no expectation of this book being an easy way to sleep

How to Marry a Muslim Girl

with any woman or to win any hearts. I want that to be made very clear.

Life as a man is difficult, it is full of struggles and challenges because that's how we grow. It takes many years of hardship until we achieve greatness. So don't be afraid of the pain, look forward to it. Eventually you will reach a stage where all those difficulties make your life so effortless.

If you use the knowledge in this book in a way other than it is intended, do not expect any Barakat in your life.

Sincerely

s.hukr

Introduction

How to Marry a Muslim Girl

You may be looking at the title of this book and thinking, sounds too good to be true. Or maybe you're thinking marriage is a joke but deep down you really want a woman in your life who loves you for you. You might be tired of chasing women or maybe you don't understand why they seem so complicated.

Whatever your case, this book is no joke. It will guide and educate you in the most effective way of marrying a Muslim woman in accordance with Islam.

Marrying a Muslim woman isn't rocket science, it's just become difficult in a world that follows culture and not Islam. It is a secret that I will teach with you in this book. I will teach you their language and how they view the world.

Consider today as your lucky day. Most people forget about the first day they embark on a new journey, but I want you remember this day.

If you are willing to spend time reading this book and applying the lessons that I will teach you. Then you will reach the goal of marrying any Muslim girl that your heart desires.

So, shall we begin?

Chapter 1
You are the Problem!

If you are truthful you will survive. If you lie you shall perish. - Khalid ibn al-Walid

How to Marry a Muslim Girl

Yes, you read that correctly.

The reason you are not having successful relationships with women is because you are the problem. Think about it. Are you a God-fearing man who is the very foundation of masculinity? Are you a disciplined man? A man with great ambitions, a man of who works and strives towards big goals? Are you a good leader, a man of justice, a man who seeks knowledge, a man who has life in order? Are you a warrior who is admired for his duty to God?

Are you following the teachings of the greatest man who ever lived? Are you aware of the stories of the great men who have lived before you? Have you learned their lessons, their teachings and follow their way of life? No, of course not.

Because if you were a man similar in any regard, you would never be reading this book. You would already have the attention of beautiful women who want you to marry them. Yes, this is a very real phenomenon.

Look at yourself in the mirror, what do you see? Is your soul happy? Are you where you want to be in life? Are you working towards your goals? Do you lie to yourself to convince yourself that you are content? Do you even know what you want from life? Is your life in line with the teachings of the

How to Marry a Muslim Girl

Quran and Sunnah? Are you a Muslim with real purpose?

Do you know who you are? Are you praying 5 times? Are you starting your day with Fajr? Are you physically fit, mentally strong and emotionally secure? Put yourself in a woman's perspective, can you even do that? and imagine how you appear?

To be successful in Deen, you must be successful in Dunya. To be successful in Dunya, you must be successful in Deen. Deen and Dunya complement one another. Deen isn't designed to limit your ability or to put restrictions on you. It was designed by Allah to give you a blueprint on how to live your best life.

The reason you are not successful with woman is because you are the problem. Your Deen and Dunya are incomplete and you are not making the necessary changes for growth.

It is an ugly truth that you need to accept. Women don't desire the person you are currently. And trust me, it has nothing to do with how good looking you are or how much money you make or how toxic your family might be. You might be nice, kind and have good intentions. But being a nice guy will not get you anywhere. You may temporarily get success with women with some miracle pickup line or a

How to Marry a Muslim Girl

fancy car or nice curly hair, but it will not yield a greater return and improve your overall quality of life.

But the good news is that you can change, you can become the Solution through shifts in your mindset and habits.

Once you accept that you are the problem, you can begin to invest in yourself. Invest in health, your passions, your social life, your wealth, your mindset… Invest in every area of your life to become a man of wealth and abundance.

But before we invest, you need to become a man grounded in faith. A man who is the very definition of being Muslim. Otherwise, you will not be able to handle the power and responsibility of wealth.

God is the most generous. How can God not give you what you want, when you are fulfilling your duty to Him and consequently to your ummah. How can God not bless you when you are trying your absolute best in His way? Impossible. Allah loves the believers.

Unfortunately, most of us do not love God the same way He loves us. We don't prioritise God in the way He should be prioritised. This is where most of us

How to Marry a Muslim Girl

go wrong in life and wonder why life is full of lemons.

You are the problem.
You need to understand that.
Accept the reality of your life.

The way you think, the way you live your life, the things you prioritise, your understanding of Deen, and your perspective of life is not optimised in such a way that you can excel.

Once you accept that you are the problem, that it is your fault for limiting yourself and not doing the difficult things required for the life you want. Once you accept this and start believing in yourself, you will then be able to attract the woman of your dreams. Only you possess the ability to change your life for the better and start working towards a solution, towards a reality that you want.

This requires you to make Dua but also put in the hard time, go through the pain, the sacrifices that you need to go through to get to where you want. There are plenty of things you know that you should be doing that you are avoiding or giving yourself false justification as to why you shouldn't be doing it.

How to Marry a Muslim Girl

For example, you know you should be going to the gym or taking care of your health through physical activity, but you are neglecting it.

You know you should be praying 5 times, praying the sunnah prayers and praying on time, you know you should be enhancing your Islamic knowledge through Islamic books or listening to Islamic lectures, but you convince yourself that you're too busy or too tired or you know enough.

You know you should distance yourself from certain friends or family members, but you still allow those people to have a negative influence on your life. These are just some common examples for you to reflect upon.

As a man you cannot expect millions of dollars to fall from the sky, you must work for it, you cannot expect to be physically fit when you don't even attempt to go the gym. Being a man is hard, it is exhausting, it is not easy. You can't avoid the pain; you must accept the pain and persevere through it.

You must be sincere with yourself, sincere with God. Sincere to your religion, otherwise life might be easy at the start but it will get harder and harder the quicker people find out that you are a liar and a hypocrite and a man of no value.

How to Marry a Muslim Girl

I know you are smart enough to understand exactly what I mean. But it's up to you to execute, nobody is coming to save you, nobody is coming to help you. Nobody owes you anything. Stop expecting from family, from friends, from people.

You owe it to yourself to start becoming the type of man that feels peace and happiness. Not because of women or your parents or what society expects from you, but sincerely for the sake of Allah. That's where you will find the most Barakat. Only expect from Allah, your loyalty lies with Him and He is the possessor of great treasures.

You must be sincere with yourself and with God. You need to stop lying to yourself, stop allowing Shaytan and his whispers to dictate your life path. To make you comfortable and easy going.

You are a man; you must regain control. Most people say they are trying their best but in reality, they are just lying to themselves to feel better. Because when you actually try your best, you get the results you want. You never give up, you never lose, you constantly try until you win.

Stop comparing yourself with people below you in performance to justify your own performance. You must look up to the greatest man to have ever lived:

How to Marry a Muslim Girl

The Prophet Muhammad, peace and blessings be upon him. He is your role model.

Once you understand and accept that you are limiting yourself and only you have the ability to overcome your own Nafs, your ego, your trauma, your internal struggles, then you can start to execute the lessons that I will teach you in the next chapter.

Chapter 2
The Grounded Muslim Man

This worldly life is like a shadow. If you try to catch it, you will never be able to do so. If you turn your back towards it, it has no choice but to follow you. - Ibn Qayyim Al-Jawziyya

How to Marry a Muslim Girl

Before we get into the real magic, there are some prerequisites that we need to meet. You must fulfill all these requirements before you even think about marriage, because these requirements lay the foundations of a healthy relationship. A healthy relationship with yourself and Allah are the backbone of any prosperous relationship.

Prerequisite 1 – Accept Islam Sincerely

You must accept Islam. You must be a real Muslim otherwise you have zero chance. Firstly, because Muslim women are not allowed to marry guys outside the fold of Islam. They are not allowed to consider hypocrites or non-Muslims. This is because Islam is the only religion whereby men are required to treat women like royalty, with respect and dignity as legislated by Islamic Law. By marrying only true and pious Muslim men, women are ensured to receive all their God given rights as they should.

Secondly, this ensures that children are raised in an environment where both parents are in alliance with each other. Both parents sharing the same ideals, ethics, morality and perspective on life. There are no petty fights or differences of opinions on major topics due to conflicting religious beliefs.

How to Marry a Muslim Girl

If you cannot accept Islam with your tongue and with your actions, then stop reading this book because you are wasting your time.

Prerequisite 2 – Do the Bare Minimum

A man is judged by his actions, not his words. If you are not fulfilling your duty as a Muslim man, no respectable lady will take you seriously. In her eyes, you will not be a suitable husband or a suitable father for her children. She doesn't have time to play games so don't waste her time.

If you aren't fulfilling your baseline duties that were assigned to you by Allah, forget about women entirely until you meet those duties with good regard. I'm talking about the bare minimum.

These duties include:

- Praying 5 times every single day, without excuse.
- Abstaining from all haram activities, including drugs, music, gambling, alcohol, smoking, immodest clothing, lying, zina, etc.
- Consistently seeking knowledge. Both of worldly and divine origin. You should be aware of the fundamentals of Islam and the rights of people. You should have a solid understanding of the Quran & Sunnah.

How to Marry a Muslim Girl

I do not expect you to become an angel, I do not expect you to become a glorified preacher like Mufti Menk, Hamza Yusuf or Nouman Ali Khan overnight, but I do hope you put consistent effort into changing your bad habits and improving your life. This may take a few months to achieve, and it will be difficult but you must adopt the mindset of "I must do what is required". Again, don't expect change to happen overnight, but make small gradual changes over time that improve and enhance the quality of your life.

Take some time out of your life, once a week or once a day on a consistent basis, whatever you can manage and invest energy into yourself. Upgrade yourself until you are able to handle the bare minimums of life.

Do you know how to communicate? Do you know how to apologise? Do you know how to listen? Do you know how to lead salah? Do you know how to make wudu? Do you know what God says in the Quran? Do you know how the Prophet lived his life?

I have put together some helpful suggestions on the next few pages that will dramatically improve your life. I will also encourage you read the book "Mumin Mindset" as it has many of the mindset shifts you need for personal growth.

How to Marry a Muslim Girl

At any time, be ready to fold the top of corner of this book and put the reading on pause until you implement each part of this book. Understanding is one thing, but implementation is another. Your implementation may not be perfect to begin with, but practice makes perfect.

The more you try, the more you strive. The more you keep working harder and smarter, more faster you will reach your every goal. Remember, I can't help you if you don't help yourself. Get comfortable doing uncomfortable things. That's what it means to be a man.

The more of a man you become, the more masculine you act. The more disciplined you are, the greater your life achievement will be in life. The bare minimums will give you a solid foundation to build your life inshallah.

Suggestion #1 - Schedule your life

If you don't already have a schedule, I suggest you create one and use each salah as an anchor point. Structure everyday around your Salah, ensuring you never miss a meeting with God.

Your time is extremely valuable, don't waste it. Money comes and money goes. People come and people go. But time comes and then it ends. You have a finite amount of time. A finite amount of energy. Don't waste it.

A schedule will allow you to manage your time in a way that is most productive. It will create a routine for you, increase your discipline, and make you accountable for yourself. You will also feel-good knowing that your days are planned and organised. You will feel a sense of achievement with each scheduled item that you fulfil, it will give you a sense of positive fulfillment and dopamine release.

Trust me, nobody likes a man who is late and has his life unorganised. It shows immaturity and a lack of discipline. If you can't be on time or early, it shows that you are not a reliable man. Trust me, it is always better to be early than to be late. Punctuality is an attractive trait to have.

You can use the calendar app on your phone or personally I suggest you use Google Calendars. You can spend some time watching a YouTube video on how to set one up. It is quite straightforward.

Suggestion #2 - Change your Wardrobe

I used to have so many different pieces of clothing, some gifted to me and some I never wore because they were buried at the back of the closet. One day, I

How to Marry a Muslim Girl

decided enough was enough and threw away all my garments that I owned. I gave them to charity.

I only kept a few clean pieces of clothing and went shopping the next day. People don't realise this, but your clothing speaks volumes. People will judge you depending on what you wear and how you wear it.

The objective of your clothing is to:

- Be Modest

- Be Simple

- Be Consistent

You cannot expect the women in your life to be modest when you aren't. And your clothing should always be acceptable for your 5 daily prayers.

You want your character to speak through your clothing. I suggest plain shirts, no logos or branding. You want neutral colours. Nothing flashy or vibrant. Long or short sleeves and made from a premium cotton or something comfortable and durable so that it lasts a long time. This is just my personal taste but adjust according to what you think is reasonable and suitable for your climate and environment.

When you find an outfit that works and suits your body structure, double down on it. Get like 5 pairs

How to Marry a Muslim Girl

of the same outfit and wear it every day. Maybe have a few different colours, like black for winter and white or grey for summer. But you want the same outfit for the next few years.

When your clothing is simple, modest and consistent, you will be put in a position where you need your character to be the most beautiful thing you adorn yourself with. It also makes you appear reliable, trustworthy and in control of your life. It will simplify your life; you don't need to waste time everyday deciding what to wear. At first you may get some backlash from the people around you or you may find it difficult to let go but don't worry about it. You need to trust the process of letting Allah guide you.

When you start to achieve your goals, you can reward yourself with more fashionable clothing items. Perhaps when you have a wife that wants to match outfits with you. But for now, stick to modest, simple, and consistent outfits.

Suggestion #3 - Cut all your Distractions

I cannot stress this enough. You must have absolute focus on your goals. We live in a time when everyone is trying to get our attention. From family to friends, from social media to work collegues.

How to Marry a Muslim Girl

Emails from random people, ads on our phone and even that occasional child crying in the background.

There is always someone seeking our attention to buy something, to do this or to do that. And let's not forget the most difficult distraction that we men face: women. I suggest that you distance yourself from all people and all sources of distractions that you encounter.

You need to have undivided focus on your goals. Delete social media if you have to, stop going out with friends to waste time, to celebrate nothing meaningful or life changing. Stop talking to women until you are in a position to negotiate terms of marriage or in a position to add real value into their life.

Stop trying to please everyone and just focus on yourself, your goals and your commitment to God. Because pleasing people will never get you far in life. Live your life trying to please God and you will get very far in life.

Write down a list of all the unnecessary things you commit to and all the things that take your attention. All the things that aren't serving you, all the things that aren't aligning with Islam. Write them all down on a piece of paper.

How to Marry a Muslim Girl

This could be playing video games that are a complete waste of time or talking to a girl that you don't intend to marry any time soon. Or spending time with friends who add no real value to your life. These are just some common examples.

Now focus on how you can get rid of these distractions one by one. Some will take longer than others but it's important that you get rid of them, they will free up your time and lessen your cognitive load.

Once you remove them, you need to replace them with healthy activities that keep you happy, allow you to reach your goals and fulfill your life purpose.

Suggestion #4 – Seek Knowledge

Make a habit of consistently seeking beneficial knowledge. Be a part of a group of friends that rewards you for being up to date on what's happening in the world. Be social with people who reward you with beneficial knowledge, who read books and attend lectures. Knowledge that helps you in this life and in the hereafter. You want to maintain a balance of knowledge about variety of things that help you fulfill your duty with Allah.

For example, you should know how money works, you should understand the concept of gold and

How to Marry a Muslim Girl

silver and why it isn't used in society anymore. Do you understand taxes and are you financially literate?

You should know how to raise children upon Deen, understand the different types of human behaviour, I recommend reading the book Surrounded by Idiots by Thomas Erikson. Can you quickly understand different emotions and people's perspectives? Why do people behave in the way they do? What are the prerequisites of raising healthy children who have the ambition to excel and succeed?

This world encourages the idea that we should be a specialist in one area of study, which is short sighted in my opinion. The best of mankind has always been multi-disciplined in a wide range of areas.

If you lose your job today or if society collapses tomorrow, do you have the abundance of knowledge to take care of your loved ones? To provide security and Rizq for them?

Do you have the knowledge to know how you will get to your goals? Do you know how to use and leverage artificial intelligence? Do you know how to use a dictionary? Do you know how to be resourceful and useful to people?

Do you know how to gift people in such a way that they value your gift and it brings them a genuine

How to Marry a Muslim Girl

smile? Do you know how to protect yourself from people who have bad intentions? Do you know what you actually want from life? Do you understand your own weaknesses and strengths?

These are just some questions for you to ponder on, for you to strive towards. To keep asking yourself questions, keep your mind active and seek beneficial knowledge. It will keep you switched on.

If you are able to, try to find a mentor who has achieved a similar life or a similar success to what you want and learn from their experiences.

You will save yourself so much time and energy when you learn from someone who is an expert in their field and who has the success that you desire. You will save many years of life when you learn from people who have already spent the time learning the difficult things that you want to learn.

For example, if you want to become a scholar, go to a successful scholar and make him your teacher. If you want to become a businessman, find yourself a successful businessman within your community that you admire and try to work for him. You want to be working with winners, not losers. You want to learn from people who are better than you and who can add a lot of value into your life in a short amount of time.

How to Marry a Muslim Girl

When you are young, broke and have plenty of time, consider working for free. A lot of people dislike this idea of working for free, but you will learn so much more than someone who gets paid to work. Because you understand that your time is the most valuable asset you have, you will be put in a position where you need to be constantly aware of everything and leverage every moment to your advantage.

So don't be arrogant, always be willing to learn, from books, from people, from family and even from people who hate you. You don't know from where you will get some useful knowledge and it will happen to change your life for the better. Stay open minded by becoming a student of knowledge and arrive at your own conclusions.

Suggestion #5 – Small Circles

Don't make everyone your friend. Be good, kind and respectful to everyone you meet but don't let them become a part of your life just because you feel lonely.

It's better to have a few good reliable people that you know, than to have hundreds of people who don't really know you and won't come to your aid when you need them.

How to Marry a Muslim Girl

Always pick your friends carefully. Their mindset will subconsciously influence you. Their actions will affect you. Only consider and choose those that bring out the best in you. Those that are reliable and will be there in your time of need. Those who have your back when times get tough. The friends you enjoy spending time with. Who bring you closer to Deen.

Those you love for the sake of Allah. The ones that can tell you the difficult truth knowing you won't like it. The ones that talk only good behind your back and confront people who talk ill of you.

Suggestion #6 – Good Character

What is good character? We all hear that a man should have good character but what does good character entail?

Umar ibn al-Khattab رضي الله عنه said

"The foundation of a man is his intellect, his honour is in his religion, and his manhood is in his character."

- Adab al-Dunyā wal-Dīn 1/17

Your character is made up of your beliefs and values which then form your behaviours and habits. This

How to Marry a Muslim Girl

influences the way you react and the way you interact with the world around you.

If you have a solid understanding and commitment to your Islamic beliefs, then you will naturally work towards habits and behaviours that display good character.

This is why you need to take some time to understand yourself and identify what you hope to accomplish with your life and who you do want to become. This will give you clarity and allow you to work towards characteristics of people who you hope to become.

In Islam, our role model is the Prophet ﷺ, his companions and the prophets that came before him. Thus, we should aspire to become like them. Allah has already chosen the great men that we should look up to and be inspired by.

Some examples of good character:

Knowing when to speak and when to stay silent. Knowing when to express emotions and when to control them. Being kind and respectful to elders, parents, and those in positions of power. To never cheat or lie to someone in trade, to remain generous and merciful.

But also knowing when to stand your ground and to fight for the rights of the poor and the weak. To be brave in the face of adversity and injustice. To be generous and patient with women and children. To remain honest even if it doesn't benefit you. To never gossip, backbite or allow others to spread rumours or negative speech.

To encourage and advise others in a way that makes them closer to the truth, not push them away entirely. To never publicly disclose secrets or sins.

Prerequisite 3 – Divine Purpose

What is Divine Purpose?

Your purpose isn't women. Your purpose isn't to please your mother, your father or to make millions of dollars. You need to understand that when things other than Allah become the centre of your heart and the centre of your attention, it will always lead to your destruction.

A man who understands that women are merely a part of their life and not the guiding force of their existence, is a man who puts God's will as his first priority in life and will be the most successful.

This is made evident by the Quran.

How to Marry a Muslim Girl

"I did not create Jin and Mankind
except to worship Me."

- Quran 51:56

Your divine purpose is simply to worship Allah. To remain loyal to your duty to God. The reason of your existence is to live a life that aligns with the instructions of the Quran & Sunnah.

That doesn't mean that you pray 5 times a day, fast every Ramadan, have a wife and some children and then expire of old age. It is so much more than that. Every human is given a gift from God. Some are naturally talented at reading, some are talented at sports, and some are given beauty, wealth, or status.

Now most people use these blessings or advantages for themselves, they are selfish. Some are completely unaware of their blessings.

But everyone has them and you must use your gifts in a way that will benefit you in the grave. You must first identify your gifts and blessings. Do a bit of soul searching, spend time with yourself until you realise what it is you want to do. Ask family, ask friends, go exploring until you identify what you are good at and what you're passionate about. These are two separate things.

How to Marry a Muslim Girl

Once you have identified what you want to do and what you are good at (your gift). You must then leverage them both in a way that would benefit the ummah in a positive light.

Another thing to point out is that your gift may not be necessarily what you want to do in life. There is a difference between wants and needs. You must focus on what you need to do, what you are required to do, not what you want to do. Once you do what you need to do, Allah will also give you what you want to do.

The greater your divine purpose, the more Barakat you will receive. I'll give you two examples of divine purpose.

Example 1: Let's say you work a retail job at the grocery, but you have a gift for food. So rather than wasting your time on social media, you spend your spare time trying to fix a problem for the Muslim community.

Let's say the problem is obesity in the older generation and they live in the west, so it can be difficult to find halal foods. Or maybe people don't have time to invest in a meal plan.

So you spend your spare time testing and creating halal meal plans. But you go a step further, you have

How to Marry a Muslim Girl

each meal plan translated in popular Muslim languages like Turkish, Urdu and Arabic. You also include some educational material explaining why health matters, a grocery list for each meal and optimise each meal plan for weight loss. Wouldn't that be amazing?

Not only are you helping people with an easy and convenient way to lose weight, but you are also addressing an issue that is affecting the community. Your intention is pure and thus there will be Barakat in it. If people are healthy, they can do more things. If they can do more things, you get the credit through good deeds and even make halal money through it.

It can become a business idea that generates passive income on the side. All because you had a genuine concern for your ummah. Not only are you proving valuable to people through your efforts, but you are also doing it for the sake of Allah. Two birds, one stone.

Example 2: You are a single father. You are good with children. You understand their needs, their wants and how to manage them. You have previously worked as a school teacher.

But you notice a problem that many children are not visiting the mosque, they are becoming distant to the

How to Marry a Muslim Girl

house of Allah. There is nothing pulling them towards Islam.

So naturally you take it upon yourself to fix this problem. You first visit the local mosques and find out the reason why children aren't coming.

Since Allah has blessed you with knowledge, you create a proposal for a playground or social area designed to attract children of all ages, that which encourages Islamic values and even has some fun educational material for children to engage in. All this is made free of charge and funded by the mosque because they love your idea.

Again, you are not doing this just for your child, you are doing it for all the children in the community. You are not doing this for the sake of money. You are doing it purely for the sake of Allah.

Perhaps this sincere gesture of yours is recognised by the daughter of the imam and she approaches you for marriage.

-

Both the above examples show how you can use your gifts to address a problem within the ummah and how the intentions must be pure. How you must stand on what's right, what's purposeful.

How to Marry a Muslim Girl

Nobody is going to tell you what to do and it will not be easy, but because you are willing to put in effort to please Allah, you will eventually be rewarded in this life and the next life.

Your divine purpose will attract you towards success in this world and in the hereafter. You need purpose in your life. You need goals, ambition, and something to strive towards.

Something other than having a wife and popping out children. Everyone can do that and does do that. There is nothing special about wanting what other people want. You must dream big. Have a fire in your heart that you want to achieve something great in your life. To leave a positive legacy. To do things that motivate and inspire people.

To stand up for what's right, to love what is right, to love for the sake of Allah. To do things in accordance with the instructions of the Quran and the way of the Prophet ﷺ. To do it against all odds, not for women, not for people, not for yourself, but sincerely for the sake of Allah. Because that's what women want, that's what women are attracted to, they love a man who doesn't make them their focus but ventures on to do what is required, what is necessary. To take the leap of faith, to maintain his honour and to be in the footsteps of great men.

How to Marry a Muslim Girl

As men, we are the role models of society and so we need to set a good example for our children to follow. You must do this sincerely for the sake of Allah. Allah created mankind as His best creation. So show the world what you can do. At least try your absolute best.

Your purpose as a man isn't just about being strong financially, physically or spiritually. It is about serving Allah in the best of manner. To use your gifts and blessings to serve humanity from a position of strength and wisdom.

If you are lost in life, how do you expect your wife to follow your lead? If you are following your forefathers that didn't achieve anything great, how do you expect to live like a king should?

When you have divine purpose, when you have the purest intention of worshipping Allah then tell me, how can Allah not make you strong? How can Allah not make you a magnet for success and power?

It does society no good to have weak men who are lost, who cannot provide financially, physically and spiritually. Who are not truthful and grounded in their beliefs and values. You must have a direction in life, a divine purpose, so that people respect you.

How to Marry a Muslim Girl

Never be afraid to speak the truth, never be afraid of making people upset by speaking what you know to be the truth. You need to hold your ground when you speak the truth because people will dislike you for it and that is your challenge.

People will curse you; they will think you are being disrespectful, mean, rude whatever rolls off their tongue and makes them justify why they shouldn't accept the truth.

Some will even distance themselves from you, why? Because the truth is bitter, it gives people a reality check that they don't appreciate in the moment, but it is necessary for their betterment. You must speak the truth and remain patient. Why? Because the patient are beloved to Allah, they will get a reward from Allah.

Being truthful comes with a price but in the long term you will yield an even bigger reward. This is what it means to be a grounded Muslim Man.

You will get a lot of hate for doing something new or different, I still do to this day. But as long as you stay steadfast on your mission, your goals, and your divine purpose, Allah will increase you in honour and respect. The journey of divine purpose will not be easy, and you will face many challenges, as did the

How to Marry a Muslim Girl

great men before you but I can assure you that it will be full of Barakat.

After you lay the foundation of what it means to be a man of God. You will remain firm, disciplined and grounded in your beliefs and values that will propel you to greatness and help you achieve the life you want.

Chapter 3
The Ideal Muslim Man

It is better to be a warrior in a garden, than a gardener in a war. - Miyamoto Musashi

How to Marry a Muslim Girl

Once you establish yourself as a grounded Muslim man, you have built the foundation of what it means to be Muslim. Now you must work towards becoming an Ideal Muslim Man, even if you never become ideal. This is the process of refinement and exponential growth.

A word of warning before we continue. Ensure that your foundations are firm, genuine and concrete. Otherwise, people will see through you and you will lose everything you have worked upon.

If the foundation is not strong, you will struggle and the building will collapse when faced with difficulties, with harsh weather. If the foundations are not strong, go back and work on those foundations until you are confident in yourself to move forward.

Nothing is more important than your reputation. You need to understand this. The last thing you want is to lose all trust and credibility because your intentions were bad or because your foundation were weak. You must guard your reputation like a man so that you appear strong and reliable. You can only do this if your foundations are strong and reliable.

Once the foundations are set, you can now build upon them and the goal is to build as high as you can to the best of your ability, according to your environment and your guidance from God.

Let's dive deeper into what it means to be an Ideal Muslim Man who is loved and admired by society. A man of power, status and wisdom; a man who follows the footsteps of the great men that have lived their life to please Allah: to reach success in this world and in the hereafter.

A man of great ambitions who will show this world through his character that Islam is the one true religion by becoming a source of value to everyone.

That is the type of man who you need to strive towards becoming and I will guarantee that if you are sincere and you put in the discipline required to follow Allah's instructions, you will remain victorious in both worlds; Deen and Dunya.

You will have the honour, the status and the power that will make you attractive to every woman who comes within your vicinity. Or at least all women who match your high integrity.

A World of Wealth

Being rich has nothing to do with your bank balance, having a nice sports car or living a lavish lifestyle.

How to Marry a Muslim Girl

Being rich has a lot to do with your friends, your connections, the internal matters of your heart and mind. How generous are you? How patient are you? How understanding and competent are you? Are you confident in your ability to survive while you are financially low, or do you get afraid and start begging other people for help? Do you get angry and start blaming your wife for not supporting you? How do you handle life at it's ups and downs?

When you are rich on the inside, you can lose everything and regain it back because you are wealthy. Wealth is what sustains you and makes you valuable to others.

Are you wealthy in your knowledge, your character, your manners, your speech… are you a resourceful man? Do you have the ability to solve problems and provide incredible value to the marketplace? Are you trying your absolute best to be the best man to your family as a brother, as a son and as member of society?

I'm asking all these questions for you to reflect upon and answer. I think you understand what I'm trying to say. The more you invest in yourself, the wealthier you will become. And the wealthier you become the more women will find you attractive. You will be

How to Marry a Muslim Girl

able to benefit yourself through your own internal reality, your family, and the community.

Women want a provider in every sense of the word. Not just in terms of money, but in every facet of life. They want a man of abundance.

A man who is overflowing with wealth from an internal reality will naturally attract women far more easily than someone who isn't. This doesn't necessarily mean you need to be a millionaire, because you can be a millionaire but still be very stingy. You can be very knowledgeable but tell your wife nothing because of deep rooted insecurities. Or maybe you have time but don't know how to spend quality time.

Imagine walking down the street and asking 10 people for $50 vs offering that money to 10 people. Giving will be met with positive emotions and creates value. Taking is met with friction and a lack of value.

This is why men who just ask for phone numbers are met with disgust. To successfully make women laugh and smile via kind speech or humorous words will be met with delight and comfort. Those men don't need to ask for phone numbers, they will just get it without asking.

How to Marry a Muslim Girl

Don't think like this: Give me your number because I asked, and I want to get to know you.

Instead think like this: I want to make her smile and ask how her day is and maybe offer to get her coffee or make her laugh, she seems to be having a rough day. Why? Because I care.

Most men take things, they don't give. Or they give but expect something in return. Or they give the wrong things that aren't valuable but instead create a lot of unnecessary friction. Your job is to give for the sake of Allah, give purely to benefit people even if it's difficult and not expect anything in return. Anything given in return is to be seen as a bonus.

Give so much free value that people love to be in your company. That doesn't mean you give so much that people take advantage of you. But give according to what you can handle and what is reasonable and most suitable. When you do it sincerely for the sake of God, there will be Barakat in it.

You must think how you can offer her value without expecting anything in return rather than constantly expressing your desire for something you want from her. Sincerity is key.

How to Marry a Muslim Girl

It's not about you, it's about her. Be a giver, not a taker. Most women will reject you because you don't offer enough value to her. You are seen from a position of weakness, not abundance. You sound needy and desperate and controlling and weird.

Some questions that I suggest you constantly ask yourself throughout your life: How much value do you give to the people around you, through your knowledge? Through your skillset? Through your manners and character? Do you light up a place when you talk about Islam?

Are you a man who is willing to read books even when you don't feel like it? Are you the type of man who will do something difficult so that you can improve your relationship with your wife, your children and your creator?

Are you a man who will do uncomfortable things because of the responsibility upon your shoulders? Or will you admit defeat and surrender and play the blame game? How much value are you prepared to give? The most valuable man will get all the attention from women and will win.

You can be a simple man, living a simple life and have simple goals. But offer so much value from an internal reality that women want to spend the rest of their life with you.

How to Marry a Muslim Girl

As a man you must constantly be investing in yourself. In your knowledge, your physical abilities, your character, you must continuously be pushing your limits, making changes when necessary and trying to achieve greatness. The more you change and improve on the inside, the more it will show on the outside.

The intention must be true. You are not being wealthy for your ego, your pride, your mother or to pick up women. You must sincerely do this for Allah. To become a better man, a better slave of God. Otherwise, there won't be any Barakat in the long term.

Pure Abundance

There is enough Rizq in this world to make every single human a millionaire. For everyone to have a palace in this world. But I still meet men who are afraid of competition, who are afraid that their Rizq will go down due to inflation, some new government policy or whatever life throws their way.

Such behaviour reeks of insecurity and a lack of trust in Allah SWT. Tell me, how can the King of Kings not provide Rizq to you while you serve him in the best of manners? How can your Rizq be decreased when you are becoming the best version of yourself?

How to Marry a Muslim Girl

My brother, Andrew Tate speaks the truth when he says people are poor because of their "brokie" mindset, their poor people mindset.

The source of nearly all unhappiness is from scarcity. Whether this be from money, resources, love, passion or even Eman. But a man who is focused on making good decisions and accepting his mistakes and growing from them, will find himself in a place of abundance.

That is what I call substance, a man with a higher purpose, who is of high value and this in turn makes him wealthy and full of abundance. Such a man walks this world with freedom and internal confidence. A man who has complete trust in himself, his lord will naturally attracts women from a place of strength.

To have pure abundance in your life, you must be a giving man. You must be generous. Be generous with your time, your wealth, your knowledge, with all your blessings. So that you can add value into the lives of others. The more you give, the more you get back from Allah.

How to Marry a Muslim Girl

Respect is Earned

Men who allow women to publicly criticise or disrespect them will never have a long lasting and meaningful relationship.

In order to hold a high level of respect and authority, you must not tolerate disrespect or injustice from anyone or anything.

Respect is earned, not given. You must earn your respect by being a high value man who is firm and upholds the values of Islam. If you are unwilling to call people out on their delusion; their bad behaviour; their hypocrisy or on values that you uphold, then you are disrespecting yourself and people will not respect you either.

You have to man up and stand up for what you believe is right even if in the moment you are perceived as completely wrong or you know that everyone will be against you. You must show people that you are not afraid of anyone except Allah. But with balance and wisdom.

This is not a free card for you to become an insensitive rude person that makes people cry and afraid. You want them to respect you, not to fear you because you are an oppressor.

How to Marry a Muslim Girl

And you will make mistakes, it's in our nature but when you realise you have made a mistake and done something you shouldn't have, this is not a moment for you to give in to your ego.

Saying sorry and apologising is not seen as weakness by women. Actually, they admire a man who can let go of pride and ego and sincerely say sorry and mean it. Remember, making a mistake will not define your life, it is what you will do after you have made the mistake that will define you. It's up to you whether you apologise, learn and grow from your mistakes and become a better version of yourself or live a life of no growth and ultimately no respect.

People respect a man who is growing, who says sorry when he needs to, who is trying his best and learning from his mistakes.

The Prophet ﷺ said,

"A believer is not stung twice by something out of one and the same hole."

- Sahih al-Bukhari 6133

This means that a Muslim does not make the same mistake twice. If you are making the same mistake over and over again, perhaps you aren't trying your best or you need to get help. You need to try different solutions until you find one that works.

Don't keep going around the same bush only to find the same problem, try something new and different, don't be afraid to challenge your belief system. To be open minded. To listen to family, to listen to friends, to listen to your haters. To those that you don't like. Be respectful to everyone even if you don't agree with them. Be respectful even if others aren't. God is always watching you and he will raise or lower your respect accordingly.

A man of Silent Actions

Men love status. They love being important.

Which is a good thing when used properly. It becomes a blessing to society. But this doesn't mean you need to tell people everything.

A man who is of high status will not tell people everything, he will show them. He will not waste his time giving people unsolicited advice. He will instead use his energy implementing his own goals and showing people that he is a man of action, a man of success, a man of excellence. This in turn will increase his respect and value.

How to Marry a Muslim Girl

People will automatically know the kind of man he is through his track record, his manners, speech and the way he carries himself.

You need to be genuine, you need to do things not to show off or to brag about to feel better amongst your friends or your family. You need to start doing good things and not telling anyone, keep your good deeds hidden from the world.

High status men will not publicly tell people how good he is, that actually makes you look like an imbecile. You keep your good actions as a secret between you and Allah. You need to guard your good deeds except that which Allah has made known to society. Made known to the honest people around you who will be your biggest supporters and ensure your integrity is kept firm.

When you are a genuine man who is real and does good for the obvious reasons, you will become the type of man that will become fluent in poetry, fluent in love and fluent in the type of man that will naturally attract women. You will be fluent in all things that women love. Because women love a man who is truthful to himself and to everyone around him. Being silent about your good deeds pays dividends in the long term. Trust me.

How to Marry a Muslim Girl

You don't need to advertise or tell people who you are, God will let everyone know through His divine ways.

Believe in Yourself

Being a man of abundance will naturally help you become more confident in yourself. It will put you in a position of strength.

But true confidence comes from believing in yourself and in your connection with Allah.

Throughout your journey in this life, you will make mistakes (just don't repeat them) and you will go through many hardships that will test you as a man. It will test your faith in yourself and in your connection with Allah.

In those moments you must believe in yourself that you will get through it, you will endure the pain necessary for growth. And you will win the battle that Allah has designed for you.

Remember, Allah sends His best soldiers to war, and you my friend are on a journey of greatness. You will feel the pain like you never felt before and at times you may feel like giving up. In those moments, you must firmly hold on to the rope of Allah and remain patient.

How to Marry a Muslim Girl

The hardship will turn to ease. You must not surrender in the meantime and admit defeat by letting go of hope.

Never get Comfortable

To be honest with you. I can't stand men who sit on the couch watching tv while their wife needs help in the kitchen or with children.

This is why I'm not very fond of culture, a lot of men will follow toxic traditions and practices because it is comfortable. I despise men like that. They are like pigs, who offer no real value to their families except whatever is expected by their culture.

They are men who can't think for themselves and are comfortable being a mommy's boy.

They are not righteous slaves of Allah. As they choose to be comfortable instead of striving towards a lifestyle as shown to us by the Prophet PBUH.

The Messenger of Allah ﷺ said,

"If Allah wills good for someone,
He afflicts him with trials."

- Ṣaḥīḥ al-Bukhārī 5645

How to Marry a Muslim Girl

Take a moment and look at our Prophet's life, it was full of uncomfortable moments, it was full of hardships and struggles. It was a very tough and difficult journey that he had to endure while being an orphan. Yet he is remembered as the greatest man to have ever lived.

Being uncomfortable is a Sunnah, we can relax when we get to Jannah. Personally, I stay away from weak men who follow culture because their energy makes me feel weak. I believe Men should never be comfortable of their own will. Men should always be working towards something.

Allah tells us in the Quran that mankind is Allah's best creation however only when we strive in the causes of Allah and do things how he ordained things to be. People often tell me Islam is complicated or that there are so many opinions, and we don't know which one to follow.

I say to those people, have you actually taken the time to study the Quran for yourself? The word to be revealed was "Iqra", it means to "Read!". Read books of knowledge and understand the fact that Allah perfected Islam 1400 years ago as mentioned in the Quran:

How to Marry a Muslim Girl

"This day I have perfected for you your religion and completed My favour upon you and have approved for you Islam as religion".

- Quran 5:3

Most people are lying to themselves, they are not working their absolute best all the time, they are not pushing themselves to be better, they are complacent being comfortable or semi-comfortable and pretend they are doing their best.

Haven't you noticed that when life is very difficult, you put in the extra effort, you make extra duas, do extra work and go above and beyond what you normally do for the sake of survival. You must apply this same survival instinct even when life isn't giving you lemons. That's what it means to be excelling.

I think Shaytan is doing a wonderful job at making the men of today's society be all delusional and comfortable in their every day-to-day life.

In the long term being comfortable will not yield any goodness for you. It will turn into regret and regret will eat you up because you will not be able to turn back time and relive your life.

As a man you will be held accountable for all your actions and you will be met with consequences for

How to Marry a Muslim Girl

when you chose to be comfortable when you knew deep down you shouldn't be. You need to understand this.

The easier you take life, being neglectful in your God given duties and responsibilities. Being lazy, forgetful, wasting time and playing around, the more this will cause you harm in the long term. Time is valuable, stop wasting it.

As a man you must be multi skilled, you must be switched on in every area of your life from family to business, to society to even yourself.

You have the ability to do many great things, you can become a jack of all trades. Allah created men with a wide range of cognitive and physical abilities. It's amazing what a man can do when he has great ambition or when his life is under threat and he is in survival mode.

A man with the mindset of "I can't" will never be able to achieve anything great. If you have this mindset you need to upgrade your belief system from "I can't" to "I will" and "I have to".

Being surrounded by men of similar mindsets will help you to keep each of you accountable and call each other out for bad behaviour and a closed-minded approach. That's how men should be.

How to Marry a Muslim Girl

Groups of strong men should constantly be working together, bettering themselves, their families and society at a large scale.

Men are the caretakers of women and to be honest with you, we are doing an appalling job of it, such that our women do not trust us. Such that they follow western ideas like feminism.

> "Weak men will marry virgins because they hate criticism. Strong men will marry widows because they love God."

The divorce rate is high and not for the right reasons and too many children have issues with their families. I know this because people come to me seeking my counsel.

They trust me, a stranger who they have never met, more than their own parents who they find it so difficult to talk to. How appalling to the fathers who have forgotten how to raise a family.

I think I went on a tangent there, but I hope you get my point. DO NOT GET COMFORTABLE.

If you follow this piece of advice, then trust me, your life will become comfortable through the inclination of people who want to comfort you.

What do I mean?

How to Marry a Muslim Girl

If you are always giving people value, working hard and being the best version of yourself, naturally people will have the inbuild desire to comfort you, to be there for you, to assist you and be at your disposable when you require them. This is how you remain a king so to speak. This is how you keep your blessings without abusing them.

Enjoy the comfort that will come from Allah not because you expected it but because you have become worthy of it.

For example. This can be from your wife who respects you and is always obedient to you, she will naturally be inclined to serve you in the best manner because you are a real man who fulfills all your duties and goes above and beyond to maintain a healthy relationship with her.

Or your good friends that have your back in times of difficulty and give you honest advice even if you don't like it. They will be your allies through the most difficult of times.

Enjoy these blessings given from Allah, they will be the sources of comfort that you need in this temporary world.

Responsibilities & Duties

How to Marry a Muslim Girl

There are so many responsibilities and duties given to men by Allah. We have more duties than women because Allah has made us the caretakers of society. We are the leaders, the breadwinners and the ones who are the most accountable by Allah.

Therefore, we must take our duties and responsibilities very seriously and meet them with good regard. Running away from your responsibilities will make you look like a weak coward and nobody like a coward.

I won't be able to cover all the duties of men in Islam but I will briefly go over 3 main topics that I believe will encompass the majority of duties and responsibilities of Muslim men. The rest you can explore in your own time by reading the book, The Ideal Muslim by Muhammad Ali Al-Hashimi. You can find it on fajrnoor.com.

Duty to God

Your connection with Allah must be firm. You must be praying every single day, 5 times without excuse, ensuring that you regularly clean your heart and constantly seek guidance through Duas and righteous people.

You must reflect upon your actions, your intentions, and your goals to see if they are in line with the teachings of Islam. Can your habits be improved? Can your knowledge be improved? What do you need to do to ensure Allah is happy with you?

Is there another sunnah that you can implement into your daily life? Is there a new Dua that you can learn? Can you improve your understanding of a particular Islamic topic?

Duty to Family

As a man of the house, you are the divine authority to ensure there is justice within the house. This doesn't mean you become a dictator; it means you handle your family in the best way you know how.

You need to know how to handle your parents, your siblings, your wife and children. Perhaps even the extended family.

You need to take time to understand people, listen to them and come up with viable solutions that become a source of Barakat. Understand their emotions, understand their intentions, their personalities and use effective strategies on how to handle and maintain people.

It is like a game of chess; you need to analyse everything within your view and make the most

How to Marry a Muslim Girl

winning plays. Win for you and win for all parties involved. That's where the Barakat is.

Be firm when you need to be and be soft when you need to be. Never allow your love for someone to blind you. Too many men love their mothers so much that they become blind. This is not fair upon your wife or sisters.

You need to know the weaknesses and strengths of every person and use this to your advantage. Work smart, not hard.

You also need to be aware of the rights of every person especially your wife, your children and the people who are under your care. You must not allow your mother, your father, your sister or your wife to cause discord or drama without reason.

You should have a very good understanding and open-minded relationship with every person in your house. This is so they can trust you with their secrets and help you establish order.

Be such a good man in your family, that every person will tell you their version of truth without hesitation. Then you use this knowledge to establish order without any bias.

How to Marry a Muslim Girl

If you can't handle your own family, what chance do you have at handling society?

Duty to Society

Assuming you are doing a good job within your family, now you must work upon your community.

Be an active community member such that you are made aware of the issues that impact society. Do the women feel protected? Are the children growing up in a good environment?

Do the men stare at women? Are people causing fitnah by having big weddings because of a lack of divine knowledge? Is the divorce rate high? Are people getting Riba based loans due to a lack of knowledge? Are there enough modest clothing shops? Is there enough places of worship for the 5 daily prayers? etc.

I think you understand my drift.

What are the issues of your society and how can you as a man be of service?

How attractive do you want to become?

There is nothing wrong with having an attraction towards women, whether it be her beauty, her wealth, her status or her Deen. But to have a high

How to Marry a Muslim Girl

success rate of marrying a Muslimah and to have success in your marriage, I will always encourage that you prioritise her Deen over everything.

When you value her for only temporary things like her beauty, wealth, status, you give her power through validation and approval that she doesn't necessarily deserve. But when you prioritise her Deen, you will be able to handle the relationship better and she will be more at peace knowing she is taken care of by a man who prioritises, principles values and morals that she also values.

Most men will bend over backwards for a beautiful woman and spend their whole lives catering to her wants. They are dominated by a woman who has not become worthy of the value you can bring as a man. Her beauty is not life changing nor is it an achievement. It is a temporary pleasure that fades very quickly and it is not enough for you to give her the world.

She may give you temporary validation and approval that you were able to attract a beautiful woman. Or it may make your ego feel good that you have a trophy wife, to feel a level of status amongst family or friends.

But you are essentially objectifying women, giving her power that she doesn't necessarily deserve and in

How to Marry a Muslim Girl

the process, lowering your own self-respect and that's not attractive. Giving her power through validation that she doesn't deserve will lead you to submissive behaviour and lead her to dominant behaviour, the complete opposite of what Allah has ordained.

For this reason alone, your relationship will not be successful in the long term. It may validate your self-worth as a man but there are diminishing returns. A relationship like that will not be the happiest one, I can guarantee it.

I want to make something clear, not all women are fake and artificial. Not all beautiful women lack real substance or character. All I'm saying is that her outward appearance has very little to do with her suitability of being a life partner. Her beauty will not solve all the problems in your life, it will not raise your children or be the comfort you need when you are going through tests and trials.

After 1 month of marriage, her beauty that you found so amazing will fade and be replaced by the beauty of the internal reality. If the internal reality is beautiful, then it is what will keep you satisfied as a man. A relationship with a woman who is internally beautiful is priceless.

How to Marry a Muslim Girl

Internal beauty can be how she listens and tries to understand you. It can be the fact that she confronts you in a respectful manner when she doesn't agree with you.

Indicators of internal beauty can be the Haya in her eyes, it can be the way she dresses modestly, it can be the way she speaks. It can be the people she hangs around with, it can be words she uses, it can be her simple lifestyle. If the internal reality is beautiful, it will be shown on the outside in some manner. You must be aware and observant to pick up on these indicators.

Can men and women be friends?

Yes and No. It depends on your interpretation of friendship. If you look at how friendship is portrayed in the west, then men and women cannot be friends. But I do believe men and women can remain allies of one another even if they are married. But with principle, with Haya and with good intentions.

> "The believing men and believing women are allies of one another. They enjoin what is right and forbid what is wrong and establish prayer and give Zakah and obey Allah and His Messenger."

How to Marry a Muslim Girl

- Quran 9:71

This doesn't mean that you talk to women every day and share your life with each while you have a wife and children. This means that when necessary and when there is requirement for you to engage with a non-mahram, you should do so in a way that is dignified and respectable.

This could be when there is an emergency, when you are at the workplace and there is a need to know your colleague, to fit in and to progress at your workplace, when you meet women in your day-to-day life.

Men and women need to communicate with each other for society to function, you cannot expect a society to function as efficiently as the western world if men and women cannot communicate and exchange necessary dialogue. A relationship – whether formal or romantic – with an Ideal Muslim is quite literally life changing.

In some cultures people think that talking to the opposite gender is haram or forbidden and that it should never happen, this is absurd. The women of the Prophet's time came up to the Prophet pbuh to ask necessarily questions about Islam and to gain knowledge. There is nothing wrong with interactions with the opposite gender as long as the guidelines are met.

You need to become comfortable talking to women even if they assume bad of you, even if they misjudge you. As long as you are respectful and don't flirt and you know deep inside of yourself that your intentions are pure. You follow the guidelines of Islam, you will survive. The truth always prevails, and you have nothing to be afraid of.

In life you need allies, you need bonds between different people, of different races and genders, so you can carry out your divine purpose. The more allies you have, the greater the unity of a people. The more resourceful you can become as a Muslim man.

Awareness

A man with a grounded Muslim mindset is very aware of his surroundings. He is aware of the things he needs to be aware of to fulfill his goals and obligations to the best of his ability.

The Prophet ﷺ said

"Seeking knowledge is an obligation upon every Muslim."

- Sunan Ibn Majah 224

How to Marry a Muslim Girl

You must be fully aware of your surroundings, your people, your culture and especially the small details. This is why seeking knowledge has been made compulsory on every Muslim.

Knowledge doesn't just refer to knowledge sought out in books or schools. It also refers to the information that is presented in your every day-to-day life. There is information everywhere. Literally.

How do people behave, how do they talk, how do they say things, are they being sincere? Are they considerate? Are they open minded?

Do they come late or early? Are they relaxed? Stressed? Do they smile often? Do they lose their temper when speaking about a particular topic?

There so many things you probably notice subconsciously when meeting new people or places, but I want you to notice and observe them consciously.

Be very aware of everything and everyone. You never know when a piece of information or knowledge can be of benefit to you or someone.

There are people who are switched on mentally because they are constantly challenging themselves, then there are others who are ignorant and lazy.

How to Marry a Muslim Girl

Being switched on comes from a having a mind that is being used. There is a reason I have so many questions in this book. They are for you to ponder about, to think about, to understand, to evaluate, to comprehend. The more you ask questions, the more you will seek knowledge, the more you process knowledge, the better your awareness and the better you will be able to interpret life.

I'll tell you right now, the ones who are aware of their surroundings will definitely be better at establishing and maintaining a meaningful connection with a Muslim woman than the one who isn't aware of the world around him.

You need to be aware when talking and engaging with women, women love it when you pay attention, proper attention and when you observe on subtle details like the new earrings she might be wearing. The fact that she seems sad but is covering it up with a smile. They like a man who can be attentive, it makes her feel loved and well protected. It makes her feel that you genuinely care and notice everything about her.

In conclusion, the better your internal reality; the better your goals; your ambitions; your actions; your character; your awareness; your knowledge etc, the better you are as a Muslim man, the easier it will be for you to attract the Muslim woman of your dreams. The intention or struggle to become better or greater should never be for women, it should always be for the sake of Allah. If God isn't happy with you, how do you expect your life to have any blessing?

I need you to read the Quran with understanding on a regular basis, this can be by yourself, through a YouTube video that goes into qur'anic topics, or even enrolling into a local class in your area. Knowledge of the Quran is non-negotiable.

Communication

Communication is a very important skill to have. Too many times things are lost in translation. We assume people are in our shoes and see life through our eyes and know exactly what we are going through. But that is hardly the case. We shouldn't have any expectations or make negative assumptions when communicating.

To become a good communicator, you must always remain in control of your emotions. Remain in control of your tongue. Don't say something out of anger or frustration and to say something without thinking. You must learn how to compose your words in an elegant manner that explains exactly

How to Marry a Muslim Girl

what you want to say. You must give people context when context is required, give people definition of words when they don't understand or assume differently to what you intended. You must listen attentively to what people are saying and how they are saying it. Learn the difference between when people are being direct and when they are being indirect.

And just because you are good at communicating, doesn't mean the other person is so don't get upset if people still don't understand you or you need to provide more clarity or you need to be patient, because you know the person is incapable of understanding

Chapter 4
Understanding What Muslim Women Want

The type of man a woman wants is someone completely different from the man they claim to desire.

How to Marry a Muslim Girl

Before I attempt to answer this question, we must journey through a woman's mind, we must understand her nature. The way women think, the way they view life and their life purpose.

You may struggle to understand the lessons that I will discuss in this chapter. So be prepared to re-read this book to get a better understanding.

Women are from the ribs of Man

The Prophet ﷺ said:

"Treat women nicely, for a woman is created from a rib, and the most curved portion of the rib is its upper portion, so, if you should try to straighten it, it will break, but if you leave it as it is, it will remain crooked. So, treat women nicely."

- Sahih al-Bukhari 3331

Most men make the mistake of treating women like their other friends. Which is quite illogical on our part. But I believe our mothers and fathers need to do a better job at raising men. So, they handle the women in their life according to Allah's degree.

You need to understand that women are not straight forward, they are not as logical as men. They are

How to Marry a Muslim Girl

emotional beings first and foremost. Which isn't a bad thing, it just requires you to handle her like a woman, not like another man.

Women are sensitive to words and sounds, whereas men are sensitive to visuals and images. Women are feminine and men are masculine, this is why we attract. We are not meant to be the same and marriage is how we choose to love each other's differences.

Women don't care what you say rather it's how you say it that she picks up on. You need to be kind, confident and respectful in your speech. You need to show that you care through your understanding of her nature. You need to say it in a manner that is elegant but also firm and respectful.

You can say I love you and mean it with your heart and you can say I love you and not mean it, you can say it without passion.

Women can sense the difference very easily and quickly. So, the more you are genuine with yourself and with Allah, the more you don't have to worry. You can just be yourself and know that your words will be taken according to your internal reality. This is why the first part of this book was so important.

How to Marry a Muslim Girl

A lot of people read my books, but they read it wrong. I admit it can be difficult to judge one's tone, pitch and the demeanour in which my words are said. But the more you stay open minded and the more you keep reading, the more you will understand and appreciate what I have to give.

It's the same with women when people try to read women and then think she is crazy, but I assure you, she isn't. She is just looking for a real man. A man who is sincere to himself and is willing to give her the love she requires from you.

The point being women are not like men, you must treat her like a woman. You must handle her with respect. Even if she is being unreasonable, annoying, and testing your patience. Allah made you the caretaker of women. Act your part.

Women are great Communicators

Women have been tasked with the duty to raise children and ensure their needs are met. This means they must be great at communicating with babies who cannot speak. This also makes them great at multi-tasking.

A woman can easily pick up body language; facial expressions, differences in speech, tone, and pitch far better than men. Women can also read between the lines; they can see hidden meaning that generally men rarely notice. This is why women talk in an indirect manner which I will cover shortly.

You need to be aware of this when you speak and engage with women. You must choose your words and actions carefully as they can tell when you are lying and when you are being honest and a man of true stature.

Women love to Talk

The way a woman releases her stress is by talking. And when a man hears a woman talk about her day and he sees problems that she has encountered, he will automatically interrupt her with a solution.

Because that's how men think, the problem needs a solution. However, I'm here to tell you that is rarely the case. Women just want someone to listen to them, agree with them (validate her) and feel like she has been heard.

She doesn't want to be offered solutions all the time, she just wants someone that cares about her to listen to her and talk to her in way that makes her feel heard, understood, and ultimately loved and safe.

Sometimes she might be excessive in her speech, being ungrateful or disrespectful and you need to ensure that as a firm grounded Muslim man, you handle her in the most mature and kind manner.

You must make it clear that you do not allow disrespect. This can be done by praising her when she does good and giving positive reminders or gentle guidance when she sways from the path.

Women are not liars

Women are indirect, they rely on indirect speech and don't always mean what they say. Women also say what they feel, their feelings can change every 5 minutes. For example, she says "All men are trash" which I think many of us have heard before.

However, she doesn't mean it. It's just a way for her to express her feelings of despair and hopelessness and maybe to get attention or validation which women crave. It can also be a bad habit of their nature.

She may use indirect speech to test your character, to see how you react, to see if you are an insecure or secure man. To see if her tiny words offend you or make you any less of a man. To see if you have complete control over your anger and lust.

She may also say "I like tall men" but may end up marrying a short king. Isn't she funny? She is trying

How to Marry a Muslim Girl

to say that she finds it attractive when a man can make her feel safe and she is silly to assume that height has a lot to do with security because I know many tall men who have cheated with another woman.

I always encourage young single men that they should talk to the opposite gender, not with bad intentions but because you will quickly learn that women are not like you and the more you engage with the opposite gender in a healthy and halal manner the more you will understand and appreciate womenkind.

Women have a language of their own, you need to understand it and learn to speak it. Your future partner will need a friend to speak with and being that friend for her will give her so much security, comfort and love. She will appreciate the lengths you go to in order to understand her nature and provide for her emotionally.

The reason women cheat, the reason they get a divorce, isn't necessarily because you can't provide financially, it most likely is because you can't provide emotionally. Being emotionally satisfied is as important as being financially provided for. This is where a lot of men fail in their duty.

How to Marry a Muslim Girl

Strengths and Weaknesses

Women are not like men and men are not like women, as we established earlier. We are similar in some regard but totally different in our strengths and weaknesses. The modern world pushes this idea of gender equality, that women and men should be forced into every part of society. Which is something that goes against the way of Allah.

There are certain roles that are better fitted to women and certain roles that are better fitted for men. I don't want to see our sisters, mothers and wives working in the mines, as a truck driver, a plumber or doing some labour-intensive job.

There is a reason why women give birth, have better multitasking ability, love to talk and make great mothers. There is a reason why women are naturally jealous, unaware of red flags in men and may struggle to understand why Allah allowed men to have up to 4 wives.

Similarly, there is a reason why men are physically stronger, make better leaders and can work every single day without needing a vacation. There is a reason why men can be aggressive, have short tempers, run away from commitment, and think about sex every other day.

How to Marry a Muslim Girl

Allah designed us to complement one another. He didn't design us to have the same abilities, strengths, and weaknesses. Frankly that would be boring, and nobody wants to live in a society where everyone is the same. A range of differences and variety are nice to have.

Women are not designed to work all day in the heat and similarly Men are not designed to give birth to children and nurture them until they reach adulthood.

That doesn't mean women cannot assist men in their God given duties, it just means that we work best and complement each other when we are doing the specific things that are our strengths align with. When we work towards our strengths, believe me, your relationship with your future wife will be better.

Women feel the World

Women see life through emotions. Attraction is an emotional reaction, not a logical decision for them. She feels attraction based upon how she feels about you. Crazy right?

It's all about how you talk to her, how your character is, how your energy is, are you immature, silly, career focused, being up to no good? Are you wanted by other women? Do you have a positive effect on the

How to Marry a Muslim Girl

world? Are you decisive, playful, understanding, respectful? How long has she known you for? Is there bad history, good history? Etc. Women take all this into consideration when deciding. This is why you should never lie to them.

What can she feel and sense about you? Is it a good feeling or a bad feeling? Does the way you talk and speak invoke an emotion of attraction or not?

> "Female attraction is not a calculated decision. It is a reaction dependant on your unconscious energy, behaviour, and character."

If you can successfully engage in a conversation where you give off all the right feelings and signals of an Ideal Muslim Man, she will feel so much trust and excitement such that her Baba will call you the next morning. Or realistically she will make herself more accessible to you so you can wife her up already.

However, when a woman feels neglected or feels that her value is not appreciated and that she has been dealt injustice, she will do things that may make her seem crazy, but she isn't crazy. This comes back to the analogy of the rib. If you do right by a woman, 90% of the time she will do right by you.

How to Marry a Muslim Girl

It all depends on your internal reality, whether your internal reality complements her reality or not. This is why two good people, who have good intentions, may still not get along and why some good people get along with bad people, ever wondered why? The goal is to complement one another, to mutually help one another, not to find someone the same as you.

In today's society, I think I speak for women when I say: young men do not care about their women and most struggle to be the embodiment of true Islam, to follow the Quran and the Sunnah with 100% effort.

Most men struggle with discipline, Haya and having outstanding character. So how can you expect a woman to feel any trust with you or to feel any level of positive attraction. If she cannot sense and feel that you are a righteous man, your chances for a long-lasting and fruitful union are very slim.

To truly fall in love with her femininity, you must learn to appreciate everything about her, even her "bad" part that drives most men crazy. You will often hear men complain about women taking forever to do her makeup or getting moody over the smallest thing like crumbs on the counter.

But the ideal Muslim Man will understand that this is all part of her beauty. He will remain unfazed by

How to Marry a Muslim Girl

such trivial things but instead enjoy the moment and use these moments to appreciate her even more.

Knowing that the reason she takes time to do her make up is to receive love and appreciation from you, not criticism. She works hard to clean the home and the crumbs on the counter may make her feel deflated after all her hard work and effort.

By complimenting her beauty after she does her make up and apologising for the crumbs by giving her affection (via a kiss and a compliment) for her efforts will make her adore you even more and fill her with joy.

This is one of the most valuable aspects of a true Muslim woman, she is a driving force for a man to be better. Appreciating and making her feel no shame or judgement for her femininity, will make her more comfortable and is the rare gift that you can give her.

True love and connection is rarely felt by women in today's world. However, in saying this, you must keep balance. Too much love for her femininity may turn into feminism and make you look like a SIMP, and we cannot allow that.

You must tap into your masculinity to ensure a union that keeps God in the centre of the relationship. We don't want an imbalance of masculinity or femininity, we want a harmonious union.

Good Women don't ask for much

We have all heard of those crazy claims girls make like 100K for mahr or a big wedding or a worldwide honeymoon trip. Perhaps she is asking that you don't marry another wife or whatever farfetched claim she is making in order to feel more secure or get validation or maybe she is signalling that she just doesn't like you.

Whatever the case, I am here to tell you the truth of the matter. Women only require a few basic things, everything else is negotiable. The more of a man you are, the more leverage you have in those negotiation talks. I think of marriage as a business deal, a union that benefits society and is the reason for Barakat within the community. But never say that to her, she will get very upset. Women view marriage as love and family, not a business deal.

So, what do women really want?

- They want to feel love and care
- They want a man who can lead her
- They want to feel safe
- They want to feel respected

How to Marry a Muslim Girl

- They want sincere commitment
- They want to feel valued and appreciated
- They want emotional fulfillment
- They want healthy intimacy

Essentially women just want pure love and to have their emotions fuelled by a man of value, a man who they adore and respect. Someone who is willing to take the time to understand her, care for her, improve her, grow with her and help her with her goals. That's her dream man.

She wants a man of responsibility, a man who she admires, who isn't lazy or has the traits of an imbecile. She wants to feel a rollercoaster of healthy emotions and in return she will do anything and everything for you.

If you treat her like she is meant to be treated, trust me, she will throw feminism down the trash and be the most obedient and loving wife you have ever met. She will cook for you, satisfy your desires, and ensure that your children are raised in a manner you deem best.

Women are designed to be obedient and submissive in their very core. They are designed to be a source of happiness for you. But don't expect any of this without patience and time. Women need time to fall in love, they need to see consistency. She can't treat you like a king if you aren't being the man of her dreams. It's that simple.

This is why you need to become a patient man, an understanding man, a man of abundance from an internal reality.

How women see love

Women see love very differently to how men see love. A man can cheat with his wife and still love her, but women will find this so difficult to believe. Because to men 'sex' isn't love, sex is sex and love is love. But to women sex is making love and to make love with another women is the worst thing a man can do to his wife.

This is why most women dislike the idea of polygyny. They don't understand how a man loves differently to how a woman loves.

Women are loved with sweet words, with kind gestures, with commitment, affection, attention. They are loved by a man doing great things for her to show that he cares and loves her. They love men with abundance, with generosity. They love men who are unique, who are good inside and 100% committed to her, who understand her feelings and give her direction in life.

How to Marry a Muslim Girl

They want romance, they want flowers, they want poetry, they want surprises. They want random gifts throughout the month that show her that he only thinks about her.

But men see love very differently. Men see love as respect, as obedience, as loyalty. We want a woman who will stay by our side no matter what life throws at us.

Men want a life partner who will listen even if she doesn't like what we are saying and take care of our needs, like our sexual needs. Men want a woman who can be quiet when he is trying to think. A woman who tries to understand him and even if she doesn't, to have trust in him to enough to know he is making the right decision. Men don't want to always communicate every thought process.

Men want a woman he can trust with his secrets, with his money and with his feelings. Men want to be loved but not in the same way as women and men don't see love in the same way as women. This is why good communication is necessary in every successful relationship.

Compliments will change her

Praise is how you change women and constructive criticism is how you change men. The feminine

How to Marry a Muslim Girl

thrives on support and praise especially from people she cares about. It is literally food for the qualities you wish to grow in her.

If you want your woman to grow in her Deen, health, happiness, love, beauty, power and depth, praise these qualities. Praise them until she exhibits them. It can be difficult to praise something that isn't there but that's what love is all about.

Treating her like another man will not work and instead will cause you problems because like I mentioned before, women are made from the ribs, you can't straighten it by being direct.

You need to learn her language, learn how to compliment her, how to praise her in such a way that invites her to change and invites her to the things you want in her.

Praise the qualities that you wish to magnify. Instead of saying "I hope you don't miss your salah." Remind her through praise by saying "My heart smiles when you remind me to pray salah on time." When speaking with woman, it is always better to call the glass half full than half empty.

Praise the tiny things, so you can make them grow. Water the seeds of what you love about her. That is how you make her change and invite growth.

Don't be Yourself

How to Marry a Muslim Girl

The worst advise I probably got was that you need to be yourself. "Be yourself and the right person will come at the right time."

This is nonsense. People aren't attracted to the person you are most comfortable being. Being yourself is basically saying, be comfortable with who you are and don't change for anyone.

How absurd and weak, being "yourself" is essentially saying be the person that your ego or nafs is most comfortable at.

Women aren't attracted to weak men who are slaves of their ego; Men who live a life of no meaning, playing video games, living in their parent's house, and engaged in a 9 to 5 job that they hate going too.

At least not the high-quality women that I speak with. Women are attracted to men who are pushing themselves to be greater. The grinders, the hustlers, the ones who are constantly struggling and striving towards a better world, a better version of themselves.

That is attractive. They are attracted to men with burning ambition towards living the best life in this world and in the hereafter. They want a role model for their offspring, a man who is unapologetic about who he wants to become and what he wants in the

How to Marry a Muslim Girl

world, a man who isn't afraid to express his desire to worship God. A man of Ihsan, a man who is continuously working towards excellence. He may never achieve perfection, but that's not the point, the point is that he is always working towards it and that's what makes him so attractive.

> "It's never about reaching perfection;
> the art is to strive for it until you become
> indistinguishable from perfection"
>
> - s.hukr

Most men give up so easily. How many men have you seen with a belly within 1 year of marriage? How many men have you seen become comfortable talking about useless topics like sports and politics that provide zero value to the people around them. They just waste their time. And then people wonder why the marriage fell apart. Why wouldn't it?

Look from the woman's perspective, wouldn't you hate to be in a relationship where your partner is living a comfortable life, and you are doing all the hard work every day and pushing yourself towards being better? It feels unfair and it feels like a lack of care and love.

As a man you can't be yourself, you must be better, you have to be uncomfortable. I'm not saying you

How to Marry a Muslim Girl

can't sleep or rest or enjoy life, I'm just saying don't get comfortable. Don't prioritise your comfort and enjoyment over your duty and purpose. There is always work that you can be doing to optimise your life and make it better for yourself, your family, and your ummah.

And by pushing yourself to be the best version of yourself is what will literally make you attractive to Muslim women. Keep the peace and you will learn to enjoy the art of winning. It is only by becoming your best self that you achieve the results that you desire.

In conclusion, what do Muslim women want? They want three things, the first is security. This means they want to be safe in your presence, to know you will never abuse her or belittle her. To know that if you ever get mad or upset at her, you will never hurt her physically, emotionally or spiritually. To feel safe in her femininity and safe knowing you will understand her, you will respect her and you will make her feel valued.

The second thing is to be provided for. Most people assume this is financially, but it also means emotional support, through your words, through your efforts and actions. They don't want money, they want to be taken care of in every regard, to the best of your ability.

How to Marry a Muslim Girl

The third thing is to be loved. The way you achieve this is by loving Allah first; by striving towards Excellence in all aspects of life; by investing into yourself, and by being a slave of Allah, the best slave. The reason why Majnun died is because he loved Layla more than Allah. Rookie mistake. Don't make the same mistake.

Chapter 5
The High Value Muslim Woman

Become such an attractive soul that women fall in love with you so damn easily.

How to Marry a Muslim Girl

Not all women are the same

Let's assume you are aware of 10 girls in your community. You probably know by now that not all are praying 5 times, not all wear modest clothing, not all wear the hijab, not all of them are cute Teletubbies that you are attracted to. But this doesn't mean they are bad people. Don't judge women so quickly because you don't know her full story. Perhaps what you dislike could be a form of blessings for you, so remain open minded.

You will find that there is a variety and variance in each person. Everyone has their unique likes, dislikes, hobbies, interests, values, thoughts, ideas and what not. There is layer of personality, a layer of experience, a layer of uniqueness in all people you meet.

There is no such thing as finding "the one" or the "perfect woman", there is only the soulmate; the right woman at the right time. The one whom you feel is the most compatible with you. The one who will complement you on your journey.

You will need to assess everything and determine whether she is good fit for you. Does she compliment you and do you compliment her? It could be that you become the encourage and love

How to Marry a Muslim Girl

that she needs to become closer to Allah. It could be that she becomes the source of happiness for you to push you to becoming a greater man.

Never pass judgement by first appearance. Always take a holistic view before determining if someone is compatible with you or not.

Ask yourself:

What type of woman do you want?
What type of women do you NEED?
What are the traits you want in her?
What are the traits you NEED in her?
What are non-negotiables?

Can you handle a woman who is wealthier than you? Can you maintain a woman who more intelligent than you? Can you keep her happy and instil a strong sense of confidence?

Do you want her to be beautiful, fun and intelligent? Do you want her to have positive emotions and make you feel happy? Do you want her to have integrity and a strong sense of confidence? Do you want to grow with her or do you prefer marrying someone older and wiser? Or do you trust Allah to guide you towards whatever is best for you?

How to Marry a Muslim Girl

Keep asking questions to yourself. It will keep you pondering. It will open your mind and heart. It will help you position yourself on how you can be the type of man who will attract the right type of woman who is best suited for you.

Be decisive on who you want to spend your life with, even if the goal is out of your reach. Even if Allah has something else planned for you. Once you can visualise the woman of your dreams, you must now strive towards it.

Have full Tawakul in Allah that he will grant you what you desire or someone better. You need to understand that you should always strive for what you want from life but if Allah decides something else, you must accept it because like Allah says in the Quran...

> "Perhaps you dislike something which is good for you and like something which is bad for you. Allah knows and you do not know."
>
> - Quran 2:216

What to look for?

You need to understand that there is a difference between lust and love. Lust is when you fall for her body, her appearance, a sexual desire, or a strong

How to Marry a Muslim Girl

appetite to engage in physical intimacy. You want to avoid lust, avoid gazing upon women and instead focus on establishing and finding love.

Love is purer, it is where you are in control and have a deep affection or warmth for her in a way that is healthy. Love comes after marriage; it takes time to build and establish but it is far more rewarding. It is the emotion women absolutely desire the most.

Women love love, they love it more than men. This is why men are better lovers; another reason why you need to be careful: will she just love the lovely things you do, or will she love you for the sake of Allah?

You need to look for women who have the characteristics and traits that will allow respect to be the foundation of the marriage. Because respect will encourage and promote love.

True love is when Allah is in the centre of the marriage. This is why you must prioritise her Deen. To find a woman who is capable of love, you need to ensure that her core values align with the principles of the Quran.

You don't need to ask her a million questions, you just need to be naturally observant and aware of her behaviour, her impact, contribution on society or to

How to Marry a Muslim Girl

her family. How does she talk, how does she think, how does she dress, how does she carry herself? Who does she hang around with? Do you see her mingling with the opposite gender? Do you see her with a private Instagram? You need to be aware and do your due diligence before you engage any further.

Her friends and family have an effect on her, even if she says they don't. They are one of the things you need to look into when considering someone for a marriage.

If you deem her attractive because her values match your own and you see a woman who compliments your energy; if you deem her a suitable partner and someone who has the foundations of a healthy marriage; then you must engage with her, not from a position of desperation but from a position of strength. We will discuss how to engage with her later.

The point I'm making is that you must do your due diligence and be aware of all the finer details, to do your research. Make a decision based on love that will last a lifetime, not lust that will expire in a few moments. To look for a woman who complements you, has respect for you and acknowledges the value you bring into her life. Make a calculated decision based on compatibility not desire, because you will spend the rest of your life with her.

How to find her?

As a man you need to be social. You need have a socially active and desirable life. Not for the sake of finding her, but for the sake of living your best life. A life of meaningful purpose, high self-esteem, confidence, and value. It doesn't matter if you are an introvert or an extrovert. Both types of people have social lives.

Introverts have deep conversations with a few people while extroverts go wide, having many surface level conversations. All humans have this innate inclination to have interactions that make us feel alive.

The easiest way to find her is to be social. Go to the mosque regularly, go to charity fundraisers, go to different events that align with your values. Be good at engaging in conversation. Feel free to let the imam of the mosque know that you're looking to get married or hint it to the brothers at the mosque, a community is supposed to help its members.

You don't need to be the man who gets the most attention, you just need to get the right attention,

How to Marry a Muslim Girl

you need to be charismatic enough that people can sense good vibes and enjoy your personality.

Being socially desirable makes you a magnet for positive vibes. It allows likeminded individuals find out about you through dialogue and free marketing via people in your social circle.

It also gives women social proof of a man who they may find attractive. But don't make the mistake of always being social. To spend all your free time being social even when it provides you zero value or worse has a negative impact on your relationship with your creator.

You don't want to be a people pleaser. Don't engage in social interactions when there is haram like gossip, shisha or other activities that jeopardise your reputation and Deen. You want to stay far away from social places of such nature for you are a great man who is looking to attract an equally great woman. If you hang around bad places, you attract bad people, and the opposite is true.

> "80% of the work is finding the right partner and 20% of the work is in keeping them."

You can try marriage marketplaces such as halal marriage apps, social media, the gym, local café's or even those WhatsApp or Facebook communities

How to Marry a Muslim Girl

dedicated to finding a spouse. It doesn't really matter what you use to find her, what matters is that you are in the right places where your social interactions are valued by you and the people around you.

You are building your credibility and reputation amongst social circles that you want to be a part of, so that when an opportunity presents itself, you are ready to make a move. You don't want to be that guy who happens to come across an attractive Muslimah who ticks all your boxes but doesn't have the confidence or social skills to pursue her, or to find out more about her. To ask for her Father's number, to engage in dialogue.

Better yet, let's say you are the lucky guy, and she comes and talks to you. What are you going to do? Panic and stutter or will you make her feel welcomed, appreciate her effort and engage in a respectful dialogue to see if you guys are compatible or not? Trust me, you do not want to be that guy who talks to every single girl he lays his eyes on, only to be rejected because deep down most women can feel you are not genuine.

Also, there is no such thing as rejection, there is only people who are compatible or not compatible. Most people who have similar foundations, will be compatible with each other. The Quran is true when it says good men are for good women and vice versa. Depending on how good you are, you will automatically cling with another good soul who compliments your energy.

Green Flags

There are many green flags that I could point out, but I will only go over my 5 most favourite ones. These are signals that can imply compatibility:

1. Religion over Culture

The biggest green flag in my opinion is a woman who is very firm and strong in her commitment with Allah. She is the embodiment of Islam, not culture. She represents her faith in a beautiful manner.

She meets all the compulsory acts of worship like 5 times salah, wearing the hijab, seeking divine knowledge, abstaining from any and all acts of haram.

This doesn't mean she is perfect, she may struggle with hijab or struggle with some part of religion but you can tell by what is apparent, that she takes religion seriously and is actively trying her best. She puts her Deen over her desire for Dunya.

She strives to work towards the sunnah and the acts of the righteous women before her. You can clearly tell that she is righteous by the way she acts and the way she talks to you. It doesn't come from a place of superiority or pride. Rather she is down to earth, and her speech makes you feel closer to Allah. She is feminine in nature and talking to her makes you feel respected.

2. Confidence

It is so attractive to find a woman who is confident in herself and her abilities. She has self-respect, self-love and complete trust in Allah to guide her to whatever is best for her.

It is not from a place of arrogance but rather it is from a place of loving herself. If she can't love herself, how can you love her?

If she can't stand up against your low-quality behaviour, how can you expect her to push you to be better. You need her to be confident, to call you out when you're not being the best husband and put you back on the right track. Inversely, you need a wife who can handle feedback and excel with it. You need her to be secure in herself and not allow insecurities to cause drama and conflict in the relationship.

You want her to believe in herself and be confident to face the world when you're not there. You need a partner in crime, an individual you can trust with all your heart to handle matters that you have left to her. To be your backbone when you need her to be.

This is why confidence in woman is attractive because insecurities do not plague her heart, she doesn't let people pull her down so easily but is resilient in the face of adversity.

3. Emotional Intelligence

It's attractive when a woman has the ability to be completely aware of her emotions and know how to manage and control them. She is in control of her emotions and not the other way around.

That doesn't mean she can't cry or turns into a robot. Instead, she has the ability to manage and maintain herself in certain situations and scenarios.

She makes life easy by knowing how to keep her emotions in check and using them to create a better life, not be an emotional wreck and create drama for no reason.

She considers both perspectives, not diverting to negativity when it suits her and not diverting to positivity when it suits her. She is unbiased and understands what she is feeling, why she is feeling it

How to Marry a Muslim Girl

and how to remain in control without allowing emotions to take hold and make matters worse.

If she can create a happy and positive atmosphere when life may not be the best of situations, she is an absolute queen that you need to wife up right now. Women like that are so rare and precious.

Emotions can either be a woman's biggest weakness or they can be their biggest strength and the fuel that makes you love her for many years to come.

Also note, women have periods, I'm not going to go into details because this isn't a biology book and I'm not your father. But essentially, it is a natural cycle of around 28 days that occurs through which a woman mood is affected. She may experience cramps, bloating and sudden mood changes. So be mindful and patient.

4. Efficient Maintenance

If she takes care of herself, mentally, physically and spiritually, it is a sign of someone who values themselves and values others. Someone who wants to work on themselves to be the best version they can be. Not in a selfish manner, but rather women need more maintenance than men. Men can sleep on the floor and have leftovers and still function without much loss in Efficiency.

How to Marry a Muslim Girl

Women need extra care, attention and comfort. They need to be comfortable because it brings out the best in them. It helps manage her emotions and her hormones and period cycles. The more maintained she is, the better she can be of help and assistance to others.

A woman who takes care of her appearance through her diet, her clothing, her ability to know when to relax and when to work out is attractive. It is even more attractive when she does it in an efficient manner. When she doesn't waste money or time at the shopping centre for something she doesn't need but just felt like buying.

She understands there is a time for shopping, for makeup, for relaxing, for self-care, for self-love, for a girl's night out and other activities that make her feel like a woman. There is also a time for her to be a wife and mother, to nurture children, to make a house into a home and to be a woman who needs to get work done: to be the glue of society.

You want a balanced woman. She isn't such a high maintenance person that she abuses your wallet every day, and neither is she such a low maintenance person that you find her unappealing. She has a nice balance and that makes her attractive both internally and externally.

How to Marry a Muslim Girl

5. Mindset

You can be educated from a university with a master's degree, and I could still consider you stupid. Education is important especially in a potential wife, something I will always encourage. But what is more important is her mindset. The type of education she has and how she utilises it.

This is very important when raising children. You have to ensure that you and your wife are on the same page and have a compatible mindset.

The way you think complements how she thinks, the way you want to live your life complements how she wants to live her life. You both have compatible goals and aspirations. There are no major conflicts which would limit you or her.

You should both be open minded, and both have the mindset of growth and achieving success in Deen and Dunya. The right mindset will help you work together and not against each other. It will help you both achieve goals very quickly, because you are both working as a team.

A couple with conflicting mindsets will self-sabotage each other. They will not understand each other's perspective, they will not trust each other, they will lose focus on what's important.

How to Marry a Muslim Girl

How to Marry a Muslim Girl

Red Flags

1. High Ego

Entitled women are very annoying to deal with. Personally, they give me a headache for free and I avoid them at all costs. You should do the same.

They are rude and ungrateful. Thinking that everything revolves around them. They need to be rejected by a high value man so that she can humble herself and understand that her inflated ego is the reason no man of substance wants to be with her. Her inflated ego is most likely due to her physically appearance, probably just thick layers of makeup with an ugly foundation. Yuck.

Her beauty should never be a reason why you allow rude or disrespectful behaviour. You want to stay away from high ego women. They might seem attractive by appearance but are the worst to be taken romantically.

2. Low Quality Friends

High quality women have a small set of friends, maybe 1-3, the most would be 5. I'm talking about real friends, friends who she hangs around with on a weekly or monthly basis.

How to Marry a Muslim Girl

You want to ensure that her friends are a positive and good influence on her. Her friends are a direct reflection of who she is. If she hangs around people who neglect hijab, neglect salah, neglect Haya then most likely she is the same as them.

And if she isn't, she is being held stagnant and down by the bad influence of her friends. They will not be pushing her potential but keeping her down with low-quality energy.

3. No passion or purpose

A woman with no passion or purpose is dangerous and of low value to you. If all she does is go shopping, watch tv shows and spend nights with her girlfriends, then marrying her will be risky for you. You don't want her to make you her purpose, nor do you want her to waste her time doing things that will not create a better life for anybody including herself.

She may say that her passion is to have children. Well, how can you raise good children when you have no education to give them. When you have zero idea of what it means to be a great mother, a great wife and a great Muslim woman.

How to Marry a Muslim Girl

She needs purpose other than having children and being a housewife. Something that she enjoys and finds meaning in.

This doesn't have to be a career or a full-time job or a big business. It can be something small that keeps her busy and she can use it to make money on the side, educate people or be a source of goodness to others. It will allow her to have skills and real-life experiences that she can use when life gives an opportunity.

4. Insecurities

Overly jealous and nosey women reek of insecurity. They have deep rooted trust issues. The type to always go through your text messages, your phone history and have no sense of personal boundaries.

Dealing with her insecurities results in unnecessary arguments that make your life miserable because she doesn't trust you the way you trust her. She loses your respect over time. This is why secure, confident women are so attractive.

Although a woman who is aware of her trust issues and is working to heal them through therapy or self-reflection can also heal in a safe relationship with a man who is genuinely trustworthy, as long as he is willing to put in the effort

How to Marry a Muslim Girl

5. Immodest Clothing

Make sure the clothing she is wearing is modest and that you discuss the hijab with her. To understand her perspective on the matter. If she is under the impression that hijab is a choice and not compulsory, then you need to move on and stay firm on your values and beliefs. Because we all know that Hijab is compulsory in Islam.

You must remain grounded on your values and uphold your religious beliefs. Because she will respect this and it may inspire her to change and to become closer to Allah.

If all the Muslim men in the world said no to women dressing immodesty. There they would have no choice but to submit to a modest way of living.

Also, just because she is wearing the hijab, doesn't mean she is a good girl, they are plenty of hijab wearing women who have boyfriends, do shisha, and other unsavoury things. Beware, optics can be deceiving.

These 5 green and red flags are some indicators for you to pick up on and assess her on. They don't tell the whole story, but you don't need the whole story. You need the introduction to decide to keep reading or not. That's it. Don't get too invested early on.

Chapter 6
How to Marry a Muslim Girl

Respect is how you attract her, understanding her will give her security and love will make her yours forever. – s.hukr

How to Marry a Muslim Girl

Now comes the juicy part of this book. The part of the book you have been dying to read. You should only be reading this part of the book if you have understood what we have discussed in the last chapter. Otherwise, go back, fight the temptation, and read the chapter again.

If you can't be honest to yourself, how can you be honest with another human being? How can you establish any kind of meaningful relationship? You owe it to yourself.

This section of the book will not be of any value to you if you have not understood the fundamental changes that I have discussed with you. If you are afraid of rejection, you are not ready to flip the next page.

How to Marry a Muslim Girl

Requirements of Nikkah

What are the requirements of marriage within Islam?

- Agreement between couple to get married
- The wali of the woman
- 2 male witnesses
- Mahr

That's it. Marriage is simple and easy within Islam. It's not compulsory to start living together immediately. You can live in each other's parents' house and work towards saving for a place of your own instead of getting a mortgage with Riba.

You don't need to invite people you don't know to a wedding you won't enjoy. You don't need to spend thousands on a wedding celebration or be older than 25 or to fit expectations of unsavoury traditions that go against the teachings of Islam.

The Prophet ﷺ said:

"The best marriage is one that is easiest."
In another narration, "The best dowry
is one that is easiest."

- Ṣaḥīḥ Ibn Ḥibbān 4163

For those that don't know, Nikkah is the practical term used for union within Islam. It is a marriage

How to Marry a Muslim Girl

contract that makes an intimate relationship between a couple permissible.

It is encouraged to get married young to avoid fitnah and also because marriage is a source of Barakat. Society needs to make marriage easy so there is less fitnah within our society and more prosperity.

As a man you don't need a job for marriage, it is not compulsory. You don't need a lot of money; you just need God and integrity. To be a man who is working towards his divine purpose. Towards becoming a man of God. That is the most valuable thing you offer in a marriage contract.

Do not expect any Barakat / blessing from a wedding that prioritises culture instead of Islam; that prioritises family instead of Allah; or prioritises your Nafs or desires instead of the will of Allah. You need to get your priorities straight.

Because as soon as you indulge into shirk or into worshipping someone other than Allah, your life will turn into chaos, sooner or later.

If you are a man firm in your beliefs, knows how to lead and to dominate, you will have no problem facing haram cultural traditions, family and what people may think of you.

How to Marry a Muslim Girl

Let me clarify something, never did I say having a big wedding is wrong, but feed the poor instead of the rich, don't put on music, don't have women dancing for the entertainment of men, don't waste your money for things that won't benefit you in the grave and don't do things that will make God angry.

Islam made marriage easy, don't make it difficult for yourself and don't let others make it difficult for you. You are a Muslim man, stand your ground for what you believe even if it is against your own family. The foundation of this ummah begins with the relationship between man and woman. Start it with Allah's blessing, not His wrath.

How to approach her?

Now that you have the foundations of a real Muslim man and understand what Muslim women want, you have the basics that will allow you to have the confidence and charisma that you need to approach her in the most dignified way that provides value and emotional security.

In this section I will discuss some ways to optimise your approach and how to secure a successful and meaningful relationship.

When engaging with her through conversation, you need to be attentive and notice signs for a healthy

How to Marry a Muslim Girl

relationship. If you overthink it and start thinking with feelings, you will fumble. You need to turn off your feelings, go and talk to her like an ordinary person and just check her vibe.

Assess the environment and just do what is the most appropriate. If you get along, Alhamdulillah, if you don't, Alhamdulillah. But not doing anything and just waiting for some miracle to drop from the sky is foolishness and cowardice behaviour.

You must try your best and then leave things in the hands of Allah. What's the worst that could happen? She says no? she says that she is already married or has a boyfriend. It's not the end of the world. It could be Allah's protection.

She isn't going to hurt you or attack you for coming up and talking to her. Just make sure you are respectful and that she can sense your intentions through your speech and character.

Women are naturally very curious, so use this to your advantage. For example, you can go up to her and ask, "Can I ask you something?"

This will most likely make her say yes and then ask any question you like, because by saying yes she has opened herself up to a conversation with you. And then you need to capitalise on this by asking the

How to Marry a Muslim Girl

right question. This could simply be, "are looking to get married?" or "where is your outfit from?" or "why do you remind me of a long-lost friend?"

Now it's up to you to assess the environment and be aware of your surroundings to say the right words, so that she finds value and comfort in speaking with you. If the intentions are pure there will be Barakat in it. The more you practice, the better you will become at this.

Inshallah you will get better the more you socialise and the more you practice, not just with women but also men. You should know how to talk with young people, old people, people from the east and people from the west. The more experiences you have, the better you will be able to approach people in a manner that brings value. This in term will make you charismatic and socially desired. It's the same way you approach her. A suggestion would be that the first interaction with her is to be polite and sincere. A bonus would be to make her laugh and smile at something that is true. You don't want to make a joke that is a complete lie.

How to Marry a Muslim Girl

Getting to know Her

Going for a woman simply because she looks pretty in a white abaya or wears white nail polish will always keep you frustrated. For this reason, you must get to know her to the extent that you can decide whether or not you see a future with her.

You must look beyond her beauty and see her for who she really is. How will she be as future mother, as a sister and as your wife?

You must take into consideration her:

- Core Values
- Fundamental Beliefs
- Behaviours
- Awareness
- Ability to perform as a Wife

When getting to know her, you must not develop any feelings, get emotionally invested or try any flirtatious behaviour with her. You must be a gentle man; you must first seek the permission of her and her Wali / family.

If you are serious, it will only takes max 2-4 weeks to get to know someone, not 8 months and then I'll think about it. You only need to ask very simple

How to Marry a Muslim Girl

questions and engage in dialogue that gives you a sense of whether she is right for you or not.

You don't need to know everything about her, and she doesn't need to know everything about you. You just need to know enough to know whether or not the foundations of a successful union are there or not. It's actually healthy to have a mystery element of someone as it creates space and room for each other to find out some details after marriage.

She is like a mysterious book; your job is to read the first few pages by asking the right questions and if you like what you hear, take the leap of faith and marry her so you can keep reading the book that you find so enjoyable and comforting.

Be a gentleman, never ask about her past mistakes, you are only allowed to evaluate her by what is currently present. It is not your job to judge her and to make her feel bad about her past mistakes. If she tells you willing this is entirely up to her and her commitment to Allah.

You are not allowed to be flirtatious when getting to know her nor to be romantic and to allow her to become emotionally invested into you before marriage. The last thing you want is to have her catch feelings for you because you were being weak and took forever to decide on whether she was compatible with you or not.

Never waste her time like that. Your reputation is on the line, you cannot engage in second class behaviour and collect a sin for a heart broken. You are in the business of winning hearts, not breaking them. Always remember that. Business first and once the contract has been signed, you can be as flirtatious and romantic as you want.

If she is not willing to prioritise your values or has conflicting values with yours, or whatever the reason may be, you must be man enough to leave her in a dignified fashion. Saying no in the most kindest way so that she still has respect for you. You cannot afford to leave a woman on a bad note no matter who she is or what she believes in.

Women talk, never give them an opportunity to talk bad about you. Never give them a reason to testify you are not a gentleman.

How to test Her?

If you're a high value man, you won't need to test her. You will be able to observe and analyse her behaviours and her speech quickly. You will be able to see if there are any discrepancies by what she says

How to Marry a Muslim Girl

and how she acts. Whether she is being a little delusional or very delusional.

You do not need to test her because you will not allow emotions to blind you. You will take the counsel of Allah and your family / friends to ensure you make the right decision and are not blinded by love.

You will make Istikhara and encourage her to do the same. The people who need to perform tests in my opinion are not high value. High value people don't have time to waste playing games. They don't have time to devalue each other by playing silly games outside of marriage.

You can play as many games as you want and have fun playing with her emotions inside of marriage when it is halal. Again, you are not in the business of breaking hearts.

She doesn't need to be picture perfect, and to have everything that you want. You just need to see if she has the building blocks of a healthy and sustainable marriage.

However, in saying this, some women will unconsciously test you. They will try to test your patience, your honesty, your leadership skills etc. Whether or not you are a grounded Muslim man with strong foundations or not. Since you are reading this book and have applied all my lessons, you will pass her tests very easily.

Be Dominant and Decisive

Don't be afraid of making mistakes, don't be afraid of being taken the wrong way. Stop caring how the world sees you. For as long as you believe in yourself and understand who you are and what you value, you will remain grounded in your decisions and appear dominant.

When making decisions, use logic first and then consider the emotional world. There is a time and place for emotions but in every day-to-day task, men should be using logic to get things done and to ensure people are taken care of.

An emotional man is often seen as weak, because he makes decisions based off his feelings. He doesn't consider all the variable; all aspects; all angles when making a decision that affects a lot of people. This is why a man who is logical and firm in his decisions is often very dominant, because he is are secure in how he thinks and in how he considers everything.

Men who are firm on their word and firm on their decisions are often disliked because not everyone understands their point of view. But they are

How to Marry a Muslim Girl

respected, because these men will make the difficult decisions required to ensure growth and to ensure prosperity.

This is why dominant men are valuable and women love a man who knows what to do and how to take lead. A man who is capable of making decisions for her in her best interest. Women may initially dislike your decision and may dislike how you seem stubborn.

However, they respect a man who cannot easily be manipulated, who cannot easily be seduced, who doesn't allow bad things to happen, who takes control of the situation and ensures nobody gets hurt.

That's why you should never be afraid of standing your ground. Never be afraid of making decisions that make people dislike you. Always remain firm and grounded on what you believe is right. It will always come back to reward you.

What I'm trying to say is to be decisive and dominant in your demeanour when considering her for marriage, if she doesn't fit your checkboxes; doesn't fit the bare minimums and you don't see her compromising on your beliefs and values, you need to move on. You need to make your decision and be content with it.

How to Marry a Muslim Girl

She will value you when you are able to make decisions for her, quicker than her and better than her. This is why women get married. They don't always want to think because it leads to overthinking. It's your job to lead her not the other way around.

When to Commit

Let's say you meet a potential through social media, through a work project or whatever and from the initial conversations and interaction, you both have a mutual interest of finding each other's company likeable. You should be able to sense it through the way she talks and communicates.

After taking the lead and doing what is required for you to get to know her better, whether that be getting permission from her father or sacrificing your lunch break to spend time with her, whatever is deemed appropriate to her.

Get to know her. The more you find out about her, the better you can decide of whether or not to commit. Get to know the basics and then drive a level deeper. Remember, be a gentleman, never ask about her past sins, never make her feel uncomfortable and never make her feel that you rejected her.

How to Marry a Muslim Girl

Always give her the disclaimer that your intentions are for marriage and that if you deem that the relationship is not compatible, then she needs to trust Allah to bless her with someone more compatible. This way she is already prepared for worst case scenario, and she won't be as upset if things didn't go the way she wanted.

> "Never feel bad about doing good things. Feel bad about bad things and having bad intentions." - s.hukr

Once you have a very good and solid understanding of who she is and what she needs, you need to decide; you cannot waste her time and your time by just playing around. You need to be decisive and either commit to her with marriage after doing Ishihara, or let her go in a dignified way. The quicker you decide, the better.

If you want to commit but you don't have a good job or the distance is the issue, or maybe her family is the problem. These are all obstacles of life if she really is the woman of your dreams and you have pure intentions, you will find a way to handle all these obstacles and make her yours.

How to Marry a Muslim Girl

Allah will guide you and make it easy for you but first you need to make the difficult decision inside yourself of whether you want to commit or not.

And let's say you committed but it didn't work out for whatever reason. You need to be content in yourself and know that you tried your best and that it was Allah's protection.

Coffee or Tea?

For you to have the most success with woman, you must be a charismatic man. One who is willing to attend social gatherings and places that are most likely to be full of high-quality individuals.

If you hang around low quality people, you will become like them and vice versa.

The Prophet ﷺ said:

"A man is upon the religion of his best friend, so let one of you look at whom he befriends."

- Sunan al-Tirmidhī 2378

Therefore, you want to be a man who is establishing relationships with high quality men and women of your society.

How to Marry a Muslim Girl

This will help you establish a network of people who can benefit you with your divine purpose but also become a way for you to find a high value Muslim woman.

If you focus on your divine purpose, you will eventually find a way to women who you admire. Soulmates have a way of finding each other, just keep working towards your God given duties.

When you happen to meet a potential partner who displays characteristics of an attractive and compatible partner, I suggest you first talk to her.

Engage with her in a kind manner to see if your soul clings with her and if she clings with yours. If the first few interactions go well for the both of you, you must be a man who is direct in your approach and seek marriage with her. This will quickly reveal whether she is still interested and whether marriage would be suitable for the both of you moving forward.

In summary, you don't need to go outside of your way to find a Muslim woman that complements you. When you are busy working upon yourself and your God given duties and purpose, you will naturally attract and be surrounded by like-minded individuals where there is mutual value and appreciation. They will have a similar internal reality to yours. When an

How to Marry a Muslim Girl

opportunity presents itself as it will many times during your life, you must take advantage of it and access her without getting blinded by emotions, and then commit to your decision.

Chapter 7
Should a Man have 4 Wives?

The Quran didn't come with a disclaimer,
'If only you're in the mood.'

How to Marry a Muslim Girl

All men have an innate desire or attraction towards women. If you don't, there is something wrong with you and you should go see the doctor because otherwise I'm going to call you GAY.

But in all seriousness, there is nothing wrong with having this natural desire for women, not just in a sexual way but also being in their presence and appreciating their internal and external beauty. Allah created women for men to enjoy, to find comfort, happiness in them and to be a source of Barakat. It is no secret that men will have Hoor Al-Iyn's in Jannah. Don't be embarrassed about it, Allah put this love for women inside our hearts.

Most women may not understand the idea of how a man can handle, maintain and satisfy multiple women. Because in reality most men do a poor job at handling the women in their life. The idea of having multiple wives is reserved for only great men, men of understanding, power, influence, or piety.

This isn't something an immature or unresponsible man should consider because it will cause more than harm than good.

The problem with men is that they will engage with women in a haram way, when they have girlfriends, "side chicks", and uphold relationships outside of marriage. That's when it becomes a problem. These

How to Marry a Muslim Girl

men need to push themselves towards greater things so they can be a source of clothing for many women who may come from difficult situations or play an important role within a community.

For example, the Prophet ﷺ had eleven wives, most of whom he married after the death of his first wife, Khadijah (RA). These marriages were not driven by lust or worldly desire, but by divine command, social obligation, and strategic wisdom.

When he married, Sawdah bint Zam'ah and Umm Salamah, he was supporting widows and orphans by supporting them emotionally and financially.

Polygyny in Islam was never about personal indulgence. The Quran itself limits it to four wives, and only on the condition of absolute justice (4:3).

Historically, it was to honour women, create strong social networks in tribal societies and allowed for strategic alliances. It also offered women protection and provision.

No matter what this world says, no matter what women say or what people pressure you to believe or think. Polygyny shouldn't be frowned upon or considered haram. It should be something we become capable of. It's not something we must commit to or exercise but rather be prepared for it.

How to Marry a Muslim Girl

"It is better to be warrior in a garden than to be gardener in a war."

If you have applied all the lessons that I have spoken about in this book so far and excel in them, you will indeed have healthy relationships with women and will be in a position of strength and abundance.

You still shouldn't consider multiple partners unless it would become a source of Barakat for you, your family and the ummah.

If you fall into the exception of being an exceptional man who can attract women easily and who understands and accepts the responsibilities associated with Polygyny, you may then consider establishing and maintaining relationships with multiple women. But, if you fear that you will be unjust and are not capable of maintaining such relationships, and that your intentions are impure, then it is better for you to stay loyal to one partner.

Polygyny is often seen as disgusting and seen as negative by many people, but usually these people may lack spiritual depth, and they don't understand the wisdom behind it. Women are also naturally jealous and so don't expect it be something easy for her. It's not something all women are capable of doing. The same way a man must build himself to be

How to Marry a Muslim Girl

great, women also have a path towards greatness that they need to work towards.

Polygyny when executed by strong masculine men who understand women, who know exactly how to handle women and who have a strong connection to God, can achieve this effortlessly and should do so if it benefits all involved. I encourage them to do so.

Not because of desire but because great men need to have a greater influencer on society, so they can make use of their extra resources and blessing that Allah has given them. One of the ways to achieve this is through the caretaking of women and having many offspring.

Islam encourages us to marry widows, to marry orphans, to marry those who have nobody to take care of them. Weak women may not understand why Allah allowed men to have more than 1 wife because they may not be spiritually strong. But equally great and high value women will understand and appreciate the reason why Allah allowed it.

There are plenty of women in the world who have nothing against the commandments of Allah if they are executed in the right way, in God's way. Those god-fearing women are waiting for men to achieve greatness in this life and in the next.

Conclusion

Congratulations on finishing this book. You should be proud of yourself. Not everyone has the discipline, the patience, and an open mind to keep reading. Now you have the knowledge, the blueprint and the masculine framework required to approach any Muslim woman you like and make her your partner for life.

I know this book hasn't gone into a lot of details or exact strategies on what to do in certain situations, but this is on purpose. You need to gain experience for yourself. Every situation is unique, every culture is different, there are so many things that you need to recognise yourself and inshallah you will.

I encourage that you re-read this book a few times if there are certain sections that you didn't quite understand or if you just need to refresh your memory. Remember, you have all the principles and lessons in this book to approach a Muslim woman and make her yours. Now you need to apply mastery. Become a master through experiences, through doing uncomfortable things and constantly putting in the work. This will enhance your character and mould you into the type of man you need to become.

How to Marry a Muslim Girl

Give your heart and soul to your vision, to your future, to your goals, to the type of man you want to become, and I am certain you will achieve it. If the non-Muslims can achieve success without God, how can you not achieve success with the help of God?

You have God, the most powerful, the most wise, the most generous, the most merciful. How can God not help you on your journey for as long as you stay loyal to Him? Impossible.

Do you want my help?

I know my words, my lessons and my knowledge have given you some aid on your journey Inshallah. It gives me great joy to know that at least one person in the world is benefiting from my books and changing their life for the better. Alhamdulilah for the opportunity that Allah has blessed me with. To Allah belongs everything and to Him we shall return. Never forget that.

Nothing gives me more joy than to know that my small little words were able to impact the world for the better. That I was able to use my influence, my knowledge and my blessings to guide people towards love. I love seeing men become their best version so they can lead women to a better future.

How to Marry a Muslim Girl

I need to see more God-fearing men in this world because it's very lonely at the top. I want to share my success with everyone, but I can't if you don't put in the effort required. I want to see this ummah build long lasting marriages, long lasting friendships and to have so much trust and faith amongst us that we don't need to sign a contract, a handshake will suffice.

I spent a very long time writing this book and making sure everything is perfect to the best of my ability. Even though I already know there will be one person who will hate what I wrote or doesn't agree or understand it. But frankly I don't care, I'm not going to let the haters distract me and neither should you.

Everything in this book will allow you to achieve your goal on how to marry a Muslim Girl. I mean it. You will get the woman of your dreams; you will find your joy and tranquillity in your life.

If you never give up, I am certain you will attain all the pleasures you desire. You must trust Allah and trust the process. You must try your absolute best. He will never let you down.

Take action today! Stop procrastinating and watch your dreams become a reality. Allah promises the

How to Marry a Muslim Girl

believers a good life in this life and in the hereafter. But he never said it would be easy.

-

I can't do it alone. I can't change the lives of other people by myself. But you can help me. If you have found any blessings from my books, I need you to leave an honest review on whatever place you purchased this book.

The more reviews this book gets, the more men I can impact and the greater the impact on the world we can have together. With your help, we can help the lives of men and women, to have successful relationships. I hope I can count on you to do your part. And follow me on Instagram @s.hukr, I love seeing people share posts about my books.

-

I am also looking to broaden my network, so if you're a brother who would like to work with me in any capacity, get in touch by introducing yourself

+61 435 319 709.

How to Marry a Muslim Girl

Thank you again for reading this book.

May Allah allow you to find benefit from my words.
May Allah inspire you to become a better man.
May Allah have mercy on you and guide you towards the straight path.

Ameen.

Sincerely,
s.hukr

P.S If you love this book, please promote it, and
share it with others and maybe you'll earn a good deed.
You should checkout my other books or maybe get one
as a gift for someone you love.

fajrnoor.com

How to Marry a Muslim Girl

21 Questions to use when getting to know a Muslim Girl:

1. What does your ideal husband look like?
2. What does marriage look like to you?
3. Where do you see yourself in the next 5 years?
4. Any health issues / debts I should be aware of?
5. What kind of wedding would you like?
6. Do you believe in second chances?
7. Do you have any non-negotiables?
8. Do you believe hijab is a choice?
9. What are your goals that you would like to achieve with your husband?
10. Do you pray 5 times?
11. How many children would you like?
12. Do you think men and women are the same?
13. Thoughts on home schooling children?
14. Would you live in a Muslim Country?
15. How is your relationship with your family?
16. Do you know the rights of the husband in Islam?
17. What does an ideal day look like for you?
18. Have you previously had any relationships?
19. What are some things you are good at?
20. What do you like to do in your spare time?
21. What makes you different from other girls?

How to Marry a Muslim Girl

S.hukr Books

1. Fajr and Noor

2. Through His Eyes

3. Noor upon Noor

4. Slice of Paradise

5. How to Marry a Muslim Girl

6. Divine Love

www.ingramcontent.com/pod-product-compliance
Lightning Source LLC
Chambersburg PA
CBHW031253290426
44109CB00012B/557